EMPOWERING WOMEN TO RISE

Find Your Voice
Build Your Dreams
And Live A Joyful Life

SPEAK AND SHINE Press

First published in Great Britain in 2025 by Speak And Shine Press.

www.speakandshinecollection.com

ISBN: 978-1-0682374-7-8

Cover by Trudie Avery.

Contents

Foreword

Kirsty Carden

It's an honour to be asked by Kier and Gill to write the foreword for this powerful book, *Empowering Women To Rise.* As someone who's deeply passionate about helping women find their voice, own their message and step into the spotlight with confidence, being part of this journey feels incredibly aligned with everything I stand for.

It's hard to believe that Speak and Shine was just an idea nine months ago — now, four incredible events later, we have this beautiful collaboration — a book written by a community of women who dared to be seen and heard.

What I love about this book is that it doesn't just share stories — it amplifies real voices. Each speaker-author has taken what they shared on stage and now gifted it to the wider world. These are stories of empowerment in its truest form — from navigating loss and claiming resilience to discovering purpose, setting boundaries, building health and rising with intention.

As someone who works with women every day to help them speak, sell and share their truth — whether on stage or online — this feels like a true embodiment of what happens when women support women and when platforms are created to help them shine.

Kier always said Speak and Shine would become a movement — and this book is living proof of that vision. It's not just a collection of stories — it's a legacy. A legacy of women using their voices to uplift and empower others.

It's been a joy to support and collaborate with Speak and Shine from the start and I know you're going to take something powerful from every single chapter.

Kirsty

Kirsty Carden
Business Mentor | Speaker |
Certified NLP Master Coach

Introduction

Kier Adair

We're beyond excited to introduce you to this First edition of *From Stage to Page* — The Speak and Shine collaboration book. A wonderful compilation of stories shared on our stage. Every author was a speaker at one of our events and we're thrilled they chose to share their powerful words wider still by turning their talks into chapters.

Everything we do at Speak and Shine embodies our values at our core — Community, Coaching and Creation. This book is no exception — championing the voices in our space and inspiring others with their anecdotes of Empowering Women To Rise.

From the beginning, it has always been about giving women a platform to be seen and heard. All stemming from a simple idea that I soon realised was needed by so many other women. Many more than I ever envisaged, as there was clearly a gap with the limited options available.

Back in October 2024, I was starting to feel my goals were slipping away. I was keen to take my message to the stage and bring more authority to what I do but found myself in a 'catch-22' situation. Whilst I had done lots of speaking throughout my career, I had nothing to show for it. To secure quality speaking gigs, I needed quality speaking assets but needed the opportunity to create said assets! The classic 'chicken and egg' scenario.

At this time, I was craving vibrant connections and threw myself into in-person networking events to surround myself with inspiring people. At one such event I was reignited, reenergised and driven to get back on my mission. After all, there were still three months of the year remaining. Maybe there was still time?

A few days later, I took a shower. A place where I am often in creative mode and can gain complete clarity. Suddenly, I knew what I had to do. If I couldn't find what I was looking for, I had to create it!

It was a very simple post on LinkedIn that day, calling all aspiring speakers. Asking anyone to respond who would like to get together, share the cost of a venue, videographer and photographer to capture our talks and share testimonials for each other. The reaction was incredible! I was clearly not the only one in this position and in no time, this little suggestion became a big deal. I now had the reason to do this, not just for me, but for everyone else who needed it too. It was no longer just about my goal to reach by the end of the year.

Riding the wave of momentum, I let it all unfold on LinkedIn. Defining the name Speak and Shine, creating the logo, getting excited about the venue booking. And yes, it was always going to be Kindred, London. The most beautiful venue that aligned with my vision to create stunning assets and gorgeous events.

Once I'd seen the traction on my post, I reached out for a second opinion from the most obvious choice for me. Whilst we had only met a couple of times, I knew she would be the perfect person to advise. The one who had inspired me with her speaking at networking events and who I already knew I would ask for help one day with my future TEDx talk. That is none other than the fabulous Gill McKay, whose response to my voice note put an even bigger spring in my step. "This has legs!" she exclaimed.

It was serendipitous that the day I called Gill, she was attending Kirsty Carden's speaking event and that even as an experienced speaker, she too was looking to create the assets I wanted. Her encouragement took my vision and belief to the next level. And whilst I continued to create the buzz with the marketing and sales pages, she designed the process to take speakers from script to stage. She became the Emerging Voices Coach and a critical part of Speak and Shine.

Looking back, it was such a whirlwind to our first Summit. It got to the point where the train had already left the station and there was no turning back. It was truly crazy going from concept to conference in less than eight weeks — what became my 'Shower to Stage Story'. But I blocked out all the noise and made a conscious decision not to overthink it as I knew my protective inner voice would say, "No! Don't do it! Don't take the risk!" Thankfully my desire to make this happen was much stronger. With Gill by my side, I felt unstoppable!

In just four short weeks from that shower and that first post, we had 12 speakers working with us and we were on our next mission to create an audience for our Emerging Voices and the most memorable occasion for all attending. With the event now at £12K, I stepped away from having a speaking slot as I knew I needed to focus on delivering over and above my vision for everyone who had taken a leap of faith into the unknown with us. My time would come soon enough.

At this point, the *Miracle Equation* from Hal Elrod[1] was my mantra — unwavering belief + extraordinary effort = incredible results, in this case creating the most magical experience for all. With the same work ethic, Gill and I were not going to stop until every 'I' was dotted, every 'T' was crossed and all the options considered. We knew it would be the attention to detail that would make the difference between a good and an exceptional event.

December 5th 2024 will be a day I will always remember. The day it all came to life and stars were born on that stage. The day I saw the power of women empowering women and doing so in a beautiful held space. The day it became clear that this was the start of not just a speaking event but a movement.

Gill and I continued to spark excitedly off each other and worked tirelessly to build the next layers of Speak and Shine.

The membership was born as a space to nurture those wanting to speak and those continuing to grow their skills.

The online Speak and Shine Connector became a monthly session as the wonderful vibe translated virtually for existing and aspiring speakers to connect.

Simply Speak and Shine was birthed to provide a more intimate space for those not quite ready for the big stage. A first step for our Emerging Voices and an event perhaps closer to my original idea of getting a few people together!

The Speak and Shine Summit then evolved into an event for more experienced speakers wanting to create the assets for their speaking careers. These speakers became the Elevating Voices.

And so, we have a wonderful flow of options for people to experience the essence of Speak and Shine. From being in the audience to taking the first step at Simply Speak and Shine, leading up to the flagship Speak and Shine Summit. It is absolutely wonderful that we've had several speakers follow this path of growing in confidence and speaking with us at both events.

The next logical step for The Speak and Shine Collection? An idea Gill and I both had scribbled down on paper — the opportunity for our speakers to build further authority and share their message. A collaboration book series was so obvious to us both, with themes to match our Speak and Shine Summits. And so Speak and Shine Press was created in February 2025.

That then brings us full circle to being beyond excited to be introducing our first Speak and Shine book, *From Stage To Page*. Enjoy reading the incredible chapters from our inspiring speakers turned authors in volume 1, *Empowering Women To Rise.*

Join us in celebrating their brilliance.

Kier

Meet The Author

Marie Fraser spent 20 years in corporate law firms, including 11 years managing a large American joint venture in London, then embraced what she calls 'the hardest job ever' — full-time motherhood. This pivot inspired reinvention as a Clinical Hypnotherapist, Female Empowerment Coach, Intermittent Fasting and Health Coach. Today, Marie empowers women over 40 to navigate the hormonal warzone of perimenopause and beyond with confidence, energy and vitality. Drawing on her unique blend of corporate resilience and nurturing wisdom, Marie guides women to become the best version of themselves when society expects decline, helping them embrace their next chapter with excitement and self-love.

From Serial Dieter To Intermittent Fasting Coach — My Journey To Self-Empowerment

Marie Fraser

Marie shares the misery and frustration of years of serial dieting and how, through a health scare, she found a way back to wellness, sustainable weight loss, renewed confidence, empowerment, vitality and feeling like herself again.

The average woman in the UK spends a staggering 21 years of her life on some form of diet, decades counting calories, weighing food like a lab technician and feeling like a failure when the latest miracle plan inevitably crashes and burns.[1]

Oh — and it will also cost her over £20,000 on weight loss products and services, slimming clubs, abandoned gym memberships, personal trainers, supplements promising the moon and exercise equipment destined to become the world's most expensive clothes hanger.[2]

I know this merry-go-round intimately because I rode it for decades.

After my last pregnancy at 38, my body staged a full-blown rebellion. Getting back to my pre-baby weight felt impossible.

It wasn't just about the number on the scales. It was the way I felt about how I looked. I felt old, unattractive and hopeless.

People would smile sympathetically and say, "It's the person inside that matters."

Bullsh*t!

When you cringe at your reflection, those words are useless. Honestly, what's 'inside' at that point is mostly self-loathing, a lettuce leaf and a couple of radishes.

By my mid-40s, desperation led me to an extreme diet just to survive a big family event. Yes, I lost weight. But at what cost? Ten months of obsessing, only to watch the weight boomerang back with interest. I felt like a failure with a side order of guilt and shame for dessert.

What no one bothered to mention was that my body was going through a hormonal warzone. I was in perimenopause, the rollercoaster leading up to menopause, when our sex hormones start waving the white flag.

There are two, sometimes three, major hormonal plot twists in a woman's life.

Puberty — think moody teenager who hates everything, especially herself.

Pregnancy — think baby brain so intense you put your keys in the fridge.

Perimenopause — think, "Who the chuff am I and why is it so hot in here?"

Perimenopause is essentially puberty in reverse, except instead of getting your period, you're throwing away tampons and watching parts of your body migrate to unexpected locations.

What the billion-dollar dieting industry doesn't want you to know is that weight loss isn't just about calories in and calories out. It's all about hormones.

An intricate hormonal system controls our bodies, affecting everything from metabolism to fat storage.

The three key players?

Insulin, cortisol and oxytocin all have a profound effect on a woman's sex hormones.

When these three are out of whack, weight gain is unavoidable and fatigue, frustration and feeling frumpy are your new normal, especially as you age.

I spent years trying to diet my way to happiness, but my body had other plans. It wasn't until a routine blood test that reality slapped me in the chops.

I was shocked and upset to be diagnosed as prediabetic and obese with high cholesterol and blood pressure, all without any symptoms. I had never married the joint pain to the excess weight I was carrying.

I felt scared. I was only just into my early 60s, with a bucket list longer than a queue at the ladies' lavatory during a theatre interval.

I refused to let my health sabotage my plans.

When my doctor enthusiastically suggested medication, I declined. I'd seen what dependence on meds had done to a family member and I knew there had to be a better way than becoming a walking pharmacy.

That's when I discovered Dr Mindy Pelz, a holistic doctor who had spent over 25 years helping women reclaim their bodies through intermittent fasting. Her approach wasn't about deprivation. It was about liberation and empowerment. It wasn't complicated — and it made sense.

Intermittent fasting isn't a diet. It's a lifestyle that involves eating during a set period of time and fasting for the rest, most of which happens while you're sleeping. There's no calorie counting, no sacrifice or starvation.

Our bodies have two fuel sources, like a hybrid car, glucose (from food) and fat (stored energy). When we eat, especially carbohydrates, our blood sugar rises and our body uses glucose for energy. Excess sugar that the body doesn't use gets stored as fat.

When we stop eating for long enough, our blood sugar drops, triggering a switch to fat-burning mode. This process, known as metabolic flexibility, is when the magic happens.

And the benefits?

Life-changing.

In December 2019, the New England Journal of Medicine published a report recommending intermittent fasting as a first-line treatment for obesity, cardiovascular disease, neurodegenerative conditions and cancer.[3]

Many studies highlighted in Mindy Pelz's book *Fast Like A Girl* also show that intermittent fasting can reduce body fat, shrink waist circumference, lower blood pressure and cholesterol, balance hormones, improve brain function, reverse prediabetes and Type 2 diabetes and much more.[4]

I started fasting using Mindy Pelz's method, so-called because women need to fast differently from men. Firstly, because we need to fast in sync with our cycle if we are menstrual as our hormones are ebbing and flowing. And secondly, if we are postmenopausal, the body needs glucose to make progesterone, the calming hormone, so it is essential to manage our glucose levels around our fasting routines.

I became my own experiment using lifestyle medicine, not pharmaceutical medicine.

After six months, and to the surprise of the doctor, my prediabetes vanished and my cholesterol and blood pressure improved.

After twelve months, I'd dropped over three dress sizes with little effort. And I've kept it off.

How?

By combining intermittent fasting with a shift in what I put in and on my body.

For years, we were told that fat was the devil and sold low-fat, no-fat products as the secret password to the healthy skinny kingdom.

More bullsh*t!

When food companies remove fat, they add sugar to make products taste good. Sugar is more addictive than a Netflix series. It spikes insulin and leads to fat storage.

The real key to wellness is good fats. The kind that makes your body and brain do a happy dance.

I started fuelling my body with good fats like olive oil, avocado, nuts and seeds.

With nature's carbs such as vegetables, whole grains and fruits.

With clean proteins including wild-caught fish, organic meat and eggs.

With nutrient-dense foods like leafy greens, fermented foods, herbs and spices.

And I stayed hydrated.

I also became a label detective. If a food had more than seven ingredients or ones I couldn't pronounce, I didn't buy it.

The truth is, sugar is the devil. It hides under 50 different names. Get to know them so they can be avoided.

I started to ask myself, "Is this good for my body and brain?" I mean, would you put petrol in a diesel car?

Women, especially those over 40, are under constant stress — work deadlines, kids, ageing parents and endless responsibilities. We are so naughty at not making ourselves a priority.

This chronic stress raises cortisol, which increases blood sugar and unused sugar turns to fat. Before you know it, your body is clinging to fat like it's the last lifeboat on the Titanic.

Many women also don't realise the impact of toxins on their hormones. Those sneaky endocrine disruptors hide in food, cosmetics, plastics, household cleaning products, contraceptive pills, antibiotics and other medications.

Years of exposure to these toxins wreak havoc on hormonal balance, making weight loss almost impossible. These toxins are referred to as obesogens.

Intermittent fasting has given me back my health, energy and confidence. It has allowed me to work with my body rather than declaring war on it every Monday morning.

Looking back at my years of dieting, the guilt, shame and self-loathing, I realised that probably around 95% of diets fail because they don't address the real issue, our hormones — something which is a priority in intermittent fasting and the *Fast Like a Girl* method.

Imagine how much kinder I could have been to myself in those serial dieting days if I'd known then what I know now.

That's why I became a certified intermittent fasting coach and am committed to empowering women who feel lost, stuck and defeated by dieting and want to reclaim their identity.

Because the struggle isn't your fault.

You deserve to feel and look like yourself again. To feel empowered as yourself.

And you can.

Without spending another 21 years trying.

Points For Reflection

What one lifestyle change (food, exercise, rest, hydration, etc) could you make today?

What one small step can you do to dampen down the stress in your life?

When was the last time you did something that made your heart sing, what was it and when will you do it again?

*"A woman with a voice is,
by definition, a strong woman."*

Melinda Gates

Meet The Author

Trudie Avery helps brilliant but hidden business owners ditch the beige and build brands that actually feel like them. As the Founder of Logolady and a Designer with over 25 years of experience, she combines a sharp eye for design, a sharper wit and a no-nonsense love for visibility. Whether she's creating scroll-stopping brand identities, mentoring creative entrepreneurs, or guiding clients through total brand transformations, Trudie's mission is clear — to turn whispers into WOWs. Her work helps business owners step into their spotlight with confidence, clarity and a brand that finally fits — like the perfect dress (with or without sparkles).

From Invisible To Unstoppable – The Power Of Brand Confidence

Trudie Avery

In this chapter, Trudie discusses how to stop being the best-kept secret in your industry and how you don't need to be loud and brash to be bold and empowered.

Are you one of those business owners who lurks in the shadows? You know, the one who is brilliant at what she does but is invisible to the people who need her. You're talented, passionate and absolutely capable — but you hesitate when it comes to showing up. You have a website but secretly hope no one finds it, a stack of business cards gathering dust and a growing sense of embarrassment around your whole brand. And as for social media? Well, that's a terrifying proposition! What do you even post? Who's going to read it? And what if — heaven forbid — someone sees it, and the tumbleweed ensues? No comments, no likes.

Does this sound familiar? Let me reassure you that you're not alone. So many brilliant business owners hide in plain sight, paralysed by perfectionism or just plain confusion. It's not that they're not good at what they do — they're incredible. But when it comes to showing the world who they are and why it matters? Total deer in the headlights.

And why is that? Because self-doubt is sneaky.

It doesn't yell. It whispers — quiet little thoughts in your ear.

"What if I don't look professional enough?"
"What if no one takes me seriously?"
"What if I put myself out there and no one cares?"

When self-doubt creeps in, we start shrinking with embarrassment, doubt and maybe even imposter syndrome.

We play small, tell ourselves branding isn't that important and convince ourselves, "If I just do good work, people will find me."

But here's the hard truth — the best businesses don't always win. It's the most visible ones that do. The ones that are clear, confident and consistent. Those who know who they're here for and show up like they mean it.

So, let's ditch the invisibility cloak, step into the spotlight and create a brand that turns heads, sparks conversations and makes you unforgettable. You need to be seen.

It's time to stand tall.

Branding isn't about being the biggest, loudest, or flashiest. It's about being you. Unapologetically, authentically you. It's about showing up confidently, owning your space and letting the world know who you are and why they should choose you.

Confidence doesn't come from 'faking it 'til you make it.' It doesn't come from wearing a power blazer or posting five times daily on LinkedIn. Absolute brand confidence comes from alignment.

When your brand feels like a true reflection of you — your values, your personality, your tone of voice, it becomes easy to show up. You don't have to remember what to say or how to act. You get to show up as the real you, a whole you, an aligned you.

A few weeks ago, a client sent me a message that stopped me in my tracks.

"I feel more like me in my business now with my amazing new brand."

And that's it. That's what great branding does. It aligns. It empowers. It creates confidence.

She didn't need a neon colour palette or a sparkly dress (though I am quite partial to one!). Her brand wasn't about being loud — it was about being true. And that truth gave her the confidence to show up and say, "Here I am." Branding isn't just how you look — it's how you feel when you show up.

Being bold doesn't mean being loud or brash. Many people think that to stand out, they have to go big. Bright colours, wacky fonts, wild taglines and over-the-top graphics.

The truth is that stand-out branding isn't about being the brightest, the biggest, the cheapest or the fastest. It's about being the most you-est version of you. Feeling confident is about you being in alignment with yourself. Feeling proud is knowing you are showing up as the best version of you.

I worked with a client recently who felt like she was constantly second-guessing herself. She kept changing her offers, tweaking her Instagram bio, switching brand colours and chasing trends. As a result, she was exhausted and completely invisible.

Once we stripped it all back and got to the core of her brand — what she really stood for, who she loved working with and how she naturally communicated, it all clicked. She didn't need to be louder. She just needed to be her.

And that's when people started paying attention. You don't have to shout to be heard. It's not about posting five times a day or appealing to everyone under the sun. It's about having honest conversations with the people you're here to help.

And that is a key question — who are you talking to, who needs you?

Let's have a quick word about niching.

People flinch when I start talking about this and I get it. It sounds restrictive like you're putting yourself in a box. But in reality? Finding your niche is the key to unlocking freedom, connection and clarity.

I recently spoke to a brilliant coach. She was highly qualified with loads of initials to her credit

— she used NLP and RTT and she had an MSc and an ICF. When working with her, she could help anyone with their business or life coaching. She could help men and women from 18 to 80 change everything from their eating habits to their career goals. She could help big businesses, small businesses and people who didn't even have a business, yet she was stumbling over what to call her own business!

I call this no man's land. Because when you try to speak to everyone, you talk to no one.

So, I dug deeper with the coach. Where have you come from? What have you experienced? Who do you understand so well because you have stood in their shoes? Who can you really help?

At this point, she started to cry. So, I waited. I knew she had just made a breakthrough.

She told me these were happy tears. The missing piece of the jigsaw had just clicked into place. She realised, in that moment, her true calling was helping survivors of domestic abuse. She had lived that experience. She had the tools, the empathy, the strength. And from that place of understanding, she could serve her people in a truly powerful way.

Suddenly, everything shifted. Her message became stronger, emotional and specific. Her offers changed. Her content changed. Her energy changed.

And most importantly, her clients found her. That's what happens when you get brave enough to own your story and serve from a place of truth.

Your niche isn't a cage. It's a calling.

Now, niching arrives in many different forms. Sometimes, it's led by who your clients are. Other times, it's about who you are, your personality, experience and skill set. Your brand is that beautiful space where who you are, what you believe in, your values and your personality perfectly align with your ideal clients. You have the same values. You care about the same things.

So, please don't dive headlong into Canva and pick a logo because you think it looks nice. Don't use your favourite colours just because you love them. Reach into the space where you look at your values — how do you want to make people feel? What do you want them to feel about you? How do they need to feel to want to work with you? Branding is all about creating a feeling. It's emotional.

When your brand feels good to you, you show up differently. You stop hiding. You stop overthinking. You stop wondering if you're doing it right and start trusting yourself. And that's when the magic happens.

If you've made it this far, I have a challenge for you — let's make a pact.

No more shrinking. No more hiding. No more half-hearted visibility.

Let's promise, right here, right now, to build a brand that feels like you. One that gives you the confidence to say, "Here I am. This is what I do. And I'm bloody brilliant at it."

Because your people? They're out there. And they're looking for you. Not a watered-down, second-guessing version. You.

So be bold. Be clear. Be honest.

And most importantly?

Be seen.

Points For Reflection

Get crystal clear on who you're talking to. If you're trying to appeal to anyone and everyone, your message will always be beige porridge. Pick a person. Picture them. Speak directly to them. This doesn't limit you — it liberates you.

Audit your current brand and ask yourself if it feels like you. Look at your website, social profiles and marketing. Do they reflect the real you or a version you think people expect? Bonus points if they all look like they belong together.

Be brave enough to invest in your brand. Your brand is the first impression, the lasting memory and everything in between. Back yourself — whether it's time, money or energy. Putting real investment into your brand isn't a luxury — it's a necessity.

Meet The Author

Rachel Mannix Fernandes is a highly accomplished Makeup Artist, Educator and Founder of Make-up in Orangeries — the bridal hair and makeup business, with over 12 years of experience. Her work spans bridal, fashion, theatre and celebrity clients, including catwalks at London Fashion Week and the BAFTA Breakthrough Brits. A former MAC Pro Team Artist, Rachel has collaborated with brands like ASOS and contributed to editorial campaigns. Passionate about education, she is a qualified educator dedicated to inspiring and developing the next generation of makeup artists through creativity, skill and mentorship.

More Than Skin Deep

Rachel Mannix Fernandes

In this chapter, Rachel reveals how her career behind the scenes in the makeup world was the catalyst that helped her find her voice, become empowered and share her face with the world.

Twelve years ago, if you had told me that makeup would one day lead me to this moment — standing under bright stage lights, voice trembling, heart pounding, followed by writing a chapter for a book, I would have laughed — a real laugh, from deep in my chest, the kind reserved for the utterly unthinkable. I wasn't someone who spoke in front of crowds or was a published author. I was the person working quietly behind the scenes, brush in hand, helping others step into their spotlight. And even as I laughed, I probably would have reached instinctively for my concealer, trying to blot away the anxiety rising to my rosy cheeks. Trying, as I had so often, to smooth over not just blemishes but emotions too.

It's funny how life works, isn't it? The very thing I thought would always keep me hidden — makeup, beauty, the 'surface' — was the same thing that taught me to step into the light and reveal my true self.

I spent years carefully crafting my career. One that kept me hidden behind the safety of brushes, palettes and other people's reflections. It was comfortable there, as I was almost invisible. I knew how to create magic for others, to hand them the tools to see themselves differently, more tenderly. But it never once occurred to me that I might need those same tools. Life, however, has a way of calling us out of hiding. It whispers to us in the quiet moments and if we are lucky — or maybe just brave enough — we eventually listen.

When most people think about makeup, they think about the surface — the colour choices and the endless churn of what's on trend and what's not.

One year, it's heavy contouring and dramatic lashes. The next, it's dewy skin and feathered brows. We are constantly being encouraged to adapt, reinvent, tweak and improve ourselves, subtly or drastically, in pursuit of a new ideal.

The beauty industry is a master at feeding this cycle. A multibillion-pound machine, it thrives on the simple, devastating idea that we are never quite enough as we are.

If you're not careful, you can spend your whole life trying to measure up to this moving target. I know I did. I fell into the rhythm of it. Perfect the skin, perfect the brows, perfect the persona. I believed that if I could just get the outside right, everything on the inside would finally settle too.

But somewhere along the way, something inside me shifted. Maybe it was the countless women who sat in my chair, each bringing not just their faces but their stories.

Perhaps it was the moments when the mascara wasn't enough to hide the grief in someone's eyes or when no amount of foundation could soften the pain in their voice.

I started to see it differently. Makeup wasn't just about fixing or masking. At its best, it wasn't about hiding at all. It was about choosing. It was about standing in front of a mirror and declaring, "This is how I want to show up today."

Some days, that meant a bold red lip and fierce liner. Some days, it meant little more than a moisturiser and a prayer. Either way, the power was in the decision, in the choice.

Every time someone sits in my chair, I see it. Beneath the foundation and blush, beyond the eyeshadow and lipstick, there's a sacred moment. A moment of trust. They are saying, without words, "See me. Help me see myself." It's a moment I have learned never to take lightly.

It's not just about technique. It's not about the perfect blend or the trendiest shade. It's about tuning in, about asking quietly, "How do you want to feel today?"

Because it's never really about the makeup. It's about how they want to feel in their skin.

It's about agency, choice and connection.

I didn't come to this work because I loved the idea of flawless skin or the latest beauty trends. I stayed because of the transformations I witnessed that had nothing to do with appearances.

A woman sits down, head slightly bowed, a flicker of uncertainty in her eyes. Thirty minutes later, she stands taller, her laughter a little freer.

That is the transformation that matters. That is what gives me goosebump moments every time I pick up a brush.

Working with makeup has always awakened the playful, creative part of me. I still get that childlike thrill when I open a brand-new palette with all those colours waiting to be explored.

The textures, the shimmer, the rich, velvety mattes — it's like stepping into a sweetshop, possibilities stretching in every direction.

But while creativity drew me in, the people have kept me here.

Over the years, I've had the privilege of being part of some of the most intimate, powerful moments in people's lives.

I've been there in the quiet, nervous hours before weddings, calming trembling hands and steadying quivering chins. I've sat with women fighting battles unseen to the world — illness, heartbreak, loss — and watched them find a flicker of strength in the simple ritual of looking after themselves. I've taught students who arrived shy and hesitant, terrified of 'getting it wrong', only to watch them leave with not just new skills but new confidence.

These moments stitch themselves into you. They become part of the very fabric of who you are. They remind you, again and again, that this work — this beautiful, messy, heartfelt work — is not about vanity. It's about dignity. It's about humanity.

I got married recently, which gave me the chance to experience this lesson from the other side.

When I announced I was getting married, the first question on everyone's lips was, "Are you doing your own makeup?"

The expectation was almost palpable. After all, I was the expert. If anyone could do it, surely it would be me.

But my answer was simple and unwavering. "No." I knew I needed to sit in the chair for once. I needed to surrender. To trust someone else to see the heart of me and to reflect it back.

And when I looked in the mirror, I saw something I hadn't expected. I didn't just see myself 'done'. I saw myself loved. I saw myself open. I saw myself ready.

The makeup was different from how I might have done it myself. It wasn't about perfecting every detail. It was about capturing a feeling, a lightness, a joy.

It reminded me so profoundly why I do what I do. Why it matters. Because, at its core, makeup isn't about perfection at all. It's about connection. It's about recognition. It's about standing in your skin and saying, "Here I am."

People often assume I'm confident because of how I present myself. They see the polished surface and think it must reflect an equally polished interior.

But the truth is, confidence, for me, has never been about not feeling fear. It has been about doing it anyway.

About showing up even when my heart is hammering in my chest. About writing words onto a page, stepping onto the stage — or into the day — with trembling hands and saying "I am here."

That is the real magic. Not flawless skin, not immaculate brows, but the quiet, courageous act of being willing to be seen.

If you take nothing else from my story, let it be this. You are allowed to glow. You are allowed to show up as your whole, beautiful, imperfect self. You get to decide whether you choose a full face of glamour, a bare face, or something in between. You get to tell the story of who you are in the way that feels right to you.

And if you ever forget, if the world's noise grows too loud and you lose sight of your radiance, remember that somewhere, someone is rooting and cheering for you.

Believing in your light, even when you struggle to see it yourself.

Twelve years ago, I would have laughed at the idea of being here, writing these words.

Today, I am living them. No concealer. No mask. Just courage. Just me. That is real empowerment — and it can be yours, too.

And you? You are more radiant than you know.

Points For Reflection

Ask yourself how you want to show up today. What is the purpose it brings you?

What can you do every day to remember your inner beauty?

How can you ensure you never lose sight of your radiance and importance to the world?

Meet The Author

Nessa O'Gorman is a High Performance Wellness Coach who has combined over two decades of corporate leadership with advanced training in holistic health. With deep insights into high-pressure environments, she helps busy people achieve sustainable performance through practical lifestyle shifts. Nessa's approach addresses the intersection of performance and wellbeing, creating a lasting transformation for leaders who want to thrive, not just survive. She co-creates personalised solutions that integrate into demanding schedules, focusing on optimisation, rather than quick fixes. Through habits that stick, she guides clients toward maximising their potential, proving that peak performance requires strategic balance, not endless hustle.

Reclaim Your Energy And Zest In A Fragmented World

Nessa O'Gorman

Nessa discusses how her journey from depletion to vitality reveals the path to sustainable performance and empowerment — and how, through practising deliberate awareness, her most valuable contributions came not by responding faster but by thinking deeper.

I still remember that day so vividly. The day I decided to step away from my much-beloved work laptop and take time to have some lunch. My husband was also working from home that day. He seemed almost surprised to see me emerge from my office before 2pm.

"You spend more time with your work colleagues than with your family," he said quietly as I rummaged through the fridge.

His words stopped me in my tracks. They were not meant to hurt — they were a mirror reflecting a truth I'd long been avoiding. I was the hamster spinning frantically on the wheel. I was the browser with fifty tabs open, each slowing down the system. I was the battery, constantly draining but never fully charging.

I looked at the clock, 12:47pm. This was the first time I'd left my desk in nearly six hours, which was typical of most days. No bathroom breaks. No water refills. Just endless Zoom calls and firefighting emails while my coffee went cold beside me.

I was trying to do it all but failing at most things and feeling exhausted. Visible to everyone except the people who mattered most, including me. And I was not alone.

Did you know that nearly seven in 10 parents admit to being distracted by their smartphones when spending time with their children?[1] In our hyperconnected world, the quality of our attention has become fractured, we've somehow become disconnected from what matters most.

How many of us recognise that hollow feeling when your child asks for five minutes of attention and your mind is racing through tomorrow's presentation? How many of us wear exhaustion like a badge of honour? And how many of us feel utterly depleted most of the time?

I started to hear this echo chamber of depletion everywhere. The mother at the school drop off, kid in one hand, phone in the other, frantically checking her emails. The executive cancelling yet another dinner with friends. That woman who can't remember her last belly-aching laugh with her besties. We've become masterful at being everything to everyone except being kind to ourselves.

This realisation launched me on a journey that transformed not just my health but my understanding of what sustainable performance and real empowerment mean. I trained as a high-performance wellness coach and discovered life-changing truths that reshaped the architecture of my life and created lasting structural change.

The first revelation was both simple and profound. Many health issues are directly tied to our everyday choices around nutrition, movement, sleep, energy and stress management and our sense of purpose. Those signals we often dismiss as normal or even ignore entirely are crucial signs from our bodies.

Modern life has created the perfect storm. We are over-stimulated, under-recovered and profoundly disconnected. We praise the hustle but penalise the pause. We celebrate output but ignore input. This imbalance takes a toll that eventually becomes impossible to ignore.

I remember the exact moment I realised I hadn't taken a real breath in months. I stood in my kitchen, shoulders hunched, jaw clenched, scrolling through emails while stirring dinner. My body had been whispering for months. But I was too busy to listen. So, it started to scream.

Something had to change. And that change began with understanding the fundamental rhythms that govern our energy.

On a typical day, we should naturally fluctuate between three performance modes — thriving mode (focused, creative, in flow, a powerful but unsustainable high output state like sprinting a marathon). Performance mode (our baseline steady state where we meet goals and manage well, forming our sustainable foundation). And survival mode (energy depleted, demands high, tasks heavy, focus fragmented — extended periods here lead to burnout).

Think of these modes as gears in a car. Thriving mode is like fifth gear. Smooth, powerful and efficient, but only appropriate at certain times. You wouldn't drive at 60 mph in a 20mph school zone, just as you can't (and shouldn't) operate in thriving mode all day long. Performance mode is your third gear. Reliable, functional, gets the job done. Survival mode is first gear, essential for getting out of tight spots, but damaging if you try to drive across town in it.

When I first mapped out my typical week, I was shocked to discover I was operating in survival mode almost 70% of the time, with brief spurts in performance mode and rare moments in thriving mode. No wonder I felt constantly drained! By redesigning my schedule to honour these rhythms, creating boundaries around email checking, scheduling focused work during my natural high-energy periods and deliberately building in recovery time, I found I could accomplish more while feeling less depleted. More importantly, I no longer collapsed on the couch every evening, too exhausted to engage with my family.

But understanding energy modes was just the beginning. The true catalyst for change was developing a practice of intentional awareness, the bridge between knowing better and doing better.

I started noticing the connection between my afternoon sugar fix and evening irritability, between a poor night's sleep and emotional reactivity and how five minutes of deep breathing transformed my ability to be present. And I learned to keep noticing.

Knowledge without awareness is just information. Awareness without action is just observation. But awareness with action becomes transformation. Like moving water reshaping stone, awareness began to carve new channels in my life. One conscious choice. Then another. Then another.

For years, I'd measured success by emails answered, problems solved, and fires extinguished. I was drowning in a sea of reactivity and felt as soon as I opened my laptop, it was akin to walking down sniper alley dodging bullets. I was always responding, never creating. Through practising deliberate awareness, I realised my most valuable contributions didn't come from responding faster but from creating space to think deeper.

This shift in perspective fundamentally changed how I approached both work and life.

I learned that sustainable performance honours our biology rather than fighting against it. I discovered that the most powerful tool is the ability to manage my energy and maintain my presence. And I found that when we show up as our whole selves, healthy, energised, present, we become visible in an entirely new way. Not just for what we do but for who we are.

The greatest irony? When I finally stopped working 24/7, my work improved. My creativity flourished when I honoured my body's signals instead of overriding them. My capacity expanded when I began treating recovery as a strategic necessity rather than a luxury.

Six months into my transformation, my daughter remarked, "Mum, you laugh more now." It was such a simple observation, yet it spoke volumes about the invisible toll my previous lifestyle had taken on me and those around me.

That is true empowerment. One year on, something has changed. And that something is me.

It can be you, too. The journey from depletion to vitality isn't about perfection or radical change.

It's about small, consistent shifts guided by deeper awareness.

Points For Reflection

Listen before the scream. Your body is whispering vital wellness clues long before it screams. Start a journal to track these whispers for just one week to reveal patterns you're missing.

Map your energy rhythms. Colour code your week into thriving, performance and survival zones, then start to redesign each day to align demanding tasks with natural energy peaks and make this a habit.

Practise intentional awareness. Set three daily alarms for 30-second pauses to take note of how you are feeling. This micro practice builds the awareness muscle that powers transformation, allowing you to notice the connections between your choices and your vitality.

"The biggest adventure you can ever take is to live the life of your dreams."

Oprah Winfrey

Meet The Author

Sharon Eden takes midlife women from, "What the hell's going on?" to being seen, heard and unforgettable, fired up by feminine influence and soul-powered presence. With over 40 years of professional expertise, a master's degree in her field, and thousands of women transformed through her work, Sharon is a trusted innovator. As the Spiritual Psychotherapist Coach, she blends ancient wisdom with cutting-edge therapeutic and coaching science in a down-to-earth way. Her Amazon #1 Bestseller, *RE-DISCOVERED*, takes you on a journey of soul transformation and has been hailed as "an achingly honest, down-to-earth, eye-opening page-turner that WILL get you thinking."

When Suicide Came Knocking — How My Wild Soul Dealt The Fatal Blow

Sharon Eden

It wasn't logic or love that saved her. In this fierce and intimate chapter, Sharon shares how a split-second awakening stopped her from ending her life and reconnected her to her Wild Soul, her unfiltered core essence.

I thought I was going to wait until my daughter went to university. I hoped she would then be out of the firing line of my husband's reaction to my divorce request because I was sure he wouldn't go quietly.

But by the time she was sixteen, I'd had it. I couldn't bear another day, let alone another two years with his passive-aggressive, conservative with a small c, restrictive energy.

A man who said NO to anything beyond what he considered normal and what the neighbours might think.

It turned out I was right.

Although I knew he was unhappy too, he wouldn't agree to a two-year divorce by mutual consent as was then current. And I couldn't sit out the five years to get a divorce without it.

So, I went ahead and divorced him on the grounds of unreasonable behaviour, the only other option at the time.

He was devastated. So devastated that, nine weeks after I requested a divorce, he began a relationship with the woman who was to become his second wife.

So, the firing line began with me squarely in the sniper's sights. And, in the midst of it all, I became ill. So ill I nearly lost my life.

As I write, I see myself as I was on that momentous evening, 46 years old, clutching a mountain of pills in my left hand and a glass of water in my right.

I was in excruciating pain from a slipped disc and could barely stand. My back and left leg were refusing to support me at a time when I needed to be strong. For, true to form, my soon-to-be-divorced husband was trying to sell our marital home from under me as I lay in my sick bed.

I was too ill to work, had no income, no safety net and no hope. The pain, physical, emotional and existential, was unbearable.

I was clinically depressed and lived in darkness, drawing the curtains against the bright rays of a glorious summer sun, which, to me, felt like poison on my skin.

I sent my daughter to stay with her grandmother and planned my suicide. Killing myself felt like the only escape from the unrelenting anguish and terror that had engulfed me.

I couldn't see beyond wishing myself gone for good.

If you're wondering why on earth I couldn't see beyond that, well, regrettably, suicide isn't rational or even a voluntary choice.

It's a psychosis, a psychological state where you lose touch with reality as you've known it and crave death. Nothing exists but the desire to wipe yourself out.

Not even a single thought of how my beloved children would be traumatically damaged by my sudden, violent departure.

So, there I was at 46. A mountain of pills in one hand and a glass of water in the other. As I began to raise the pills to my mouth, I was oblivious to the reality of what I was doing.

As if in slow motion, I watched my hand getting closer and closer and closer, my lips parting to receive those sweet, sweet releasing pills.

And then, out of nowhere, I heard a yell. Not a voice outside me but a thundering roar inside my head...NOOOOOOOO!

At that moment, I saw a flash, a nanosecond vision of a pop group I couldn't name and a song I couldn't hear. Yet, paradoxically, they stopped me in my tracks.

ENOUGH!

The pills cascaded from my hand and the glass shattered on the floor. Somehow, I managed to get through the night and, early next morning, got the help I needed to keep me here.

Many years later, telling a friend about how I nearly killed myself, I suddenly realised that the pop group was The Communards from the 1980s.

And the song?

If you know of The Communards, you might already have guessed. It was, of course, "Don't Leave Me This Way."

It's a heartfelt plea from the singer to a beloved, begging them not to leave, as life would be unliveable in the absence of love.

What an extraordinarily brilliant message to stop my self-killing chaos.

Some would say it came from God or the Goddess, a guardian angel, a spirit guide, or some otherworldly entity. But it was none of these for me.

The message in my head came as an auditory and visual phenomenon, which felt acutely personal. It was a 100% down-and-dirty, here-on-earth plea to keep me physically alive.

A plea which I believe came from my Wild Soul, which can't exist without the space suit of my body and personality through which to express.

My Wild Soul is the part of me that remembers who I genuinely am, even when the rest of me forgets.

The part of me that saw through the darkness and refused to let me go.

The part of me that dealt the fatal blow to suicide when it came knocking at my door.

So, what on earth is a Wild Soul?

Your Wild Soul is the spark of the divine within you. Its sacred essence holds the blueprint of who you were designed to be, who you really are before the world taught you otherwise.

A blueprint that outlines your full potential, untrammelled by social conditioning.

Imagine arriving in the womb pre-programmed to be the most humane, loving and collaborative being you could ever be. A being with all the knowledge and wisdom to be able to create heaven here on earth.

But, as an old rabbinical story tells us, an angel kisses you on the cheek at the moment of birth and you forget who you really are, only to spend the rest of your life trying to remember!

Your Wild Soul calls to you through your pain, your longings and even your daily life to help you reclaim who you really are. It urges you to remember who you're meant to be and calls you to look within and evolve into even more of your birthright, your magnificence.

When clients work with me, the pain, problem or challenge they bring is a clue to what of their unexpressed potential is trying to come through. I work personality to personality to resolve their issue.

And there's more, much more.

I also work Wild Soul to Wild Soul, helping my clients take their next evolutionary step through their concerns and resolutions to become even more of who they really are.

And who they, you and I really are isn't some nebulous construct, even if it sounds like it. Indeed, it's been suggested that we're all spiritual beings having a human experience in order to develop ourselves into the best we can be for the highest good and our own.

You'll know how it is to have moments of awe, a spiritual experience.

You might have experienced them in a beautiful place in nature, the sun rising or setting, a moment of deep connection between you and a loved one, holding a newborn baby, looking into its eyes, or even in prayer or worship.

I once had such a moment seeing a delicious vase in a shop window. Its curvaceous shape and colours were beyond beautiful and in those seconds, I was transported out of my everyday experience.

In fact, neuroscience has shown that certain areas of the brain light up when we have spiritual 'happenings'. Research findings even suggest that spirituality is innate and that we're hardwired for it.[1]

So, who you really are isn't some nebulous construct.

In addition to holding your original design, your Wild Soul is your North Star and compass. It knows exactly what's right for you and what's not. If you listen to its inner wisdom, decision-making becomes an absolute no-brainer.

I wish I'd known that before I married my ex, as it would have saved us both loads of aggravation. But, hey, that's a whole other story!

So, why does connecting to your Wild Soul matter now?

Well, apart from the not-inconsequential matter of your sacred evolution, we live in troubled times.

There's the rise of the extreme right with its hatred and divisiveness, an epidemic of natural disasters linked to climate change, wars and political and socio-economic mayhem at every turn.

Plus, at a more personal level, where would we women be without having to deal with abuses of the patriarchy, misogyny and sexism?

However, there is hope...

If my wondrous Wild Soul could stop me from killing myself, imagine what our collective Wild Souls could do for humanity and planet Earth. What could we achieve if we all listened to their sacred integrity and loving wisdom?

For our Wild Souls know how to create, how to heal and how to unite.

They know exactly how to live here on earth as a collaborative, interdependent and loving energy aligned with the highest good for all beings and all things.

And, if my Wild Soul could save my life, just imagine what your Wild Soul could do for you...

Points For Reflection

When have you experienced feelings of awe and what learning did they bring or could have brought you?

In what way or ways, however big or small, might your Wild Soul have saved you?

If you were connected with your Wild Soul, its integrity and loving wisdom, how would your life be improved?

"Courage starts with showing up and letting ourselves be seen."

Brené Brown

Meet The Author

Caz Hawley is known as The Change Empowerment Coach and is a well-recognised Executive Leadership and Career Coach and best-selling author on a mission to build the UK's most empowering and supportive Coaching for Change Acceleration Hub for people ready to rise. After decades in people management, including 18 years as a Professional Coach, she has seen hundreds of talented, gifted people find change hard and fearful, paralysing the impact they can make. She now provides the coaching, tools, courses and resources they need to build resilience, reputation and readiness at every level, keeping people at the heart of change and transformation.

Empowering Change Through Visibility, Voice And Choice

Caz Hawley

In this chapter, Caz asks probing questions to help us understand how to show up empowered and aligned during challenging times of change.

Have you ever wondered how to feel more empowered during times of change? Or how to regain a sense of control when it feels like change has you in a vice-like grip?

Have you ever paused to ask yourself, "Where am I now and where do I want to be?"

Asking these questions of myself has been transformative in my life and work. Here, I'll share aspects from my story where the answers helped me move forward with clarity and courage. And they can for you too.

Maybe, like me, you've experienced major upheaval at work or home. Perhaps you're in transition, caught in limbo, grieving what was and unsure of what's next. Maybe you dislike change altogether because it feels imposed on you — uncomfortable, unwelcome, unchosen.

Or perhaps you feel ready to change but feel silenced or stuck. Your light feels dimmed and you wonder if it will ever shine again.

So now ask yourself, "Where do I want to be instead?"

Imagine feeling bolder and more visible in times of uncertainty. Picture yourself stepping into the unknown with confidence and conviction. Hear your voice — a clear, strong, confident compass guiding you and others through change. Your words carry weight. They matter. They are trustworthy.

If any of this resonates with you, the next question becomes, "How do we navigate change without losing our visibility or sense of self?"

The truth is that change can shake us and push us into discomfort. It stirs up vulnerability. It invites self-doubt. And in those moments, it's easy to shrink, silence ourselves and disappear.

But what if you did the opposite?

Because when change hits, we always have a choice. To fade into the background — or to step forward and be seen.

I believe change doesn't always have to be hard. And even when it is, we can find empowerment in how we respond.

Let me take you on a journey back to the 1980s. I was fifteen when I was diagnosed with scoliosis — a severe curvature of the spine. Instead of sitting my exams, I spent months in hospital undergoing spinal surgery, followed by six months in a full torso plaster cast (not exactly a fashion statement!). After that, I wore a surgical corset brace for another eight months.

Needless to say, I missed key years of my social and educational development.

Everything changed — my physical strength weakened, my self-image shifted, and my confidence took a hit. "How can I hide?" I often wondered. (Tricky when you're wearing a humongous cast!)

At first, it felt like change was happening to me and I had no idea how to navigate this.

But over time, I realised I still had a choice. I could let this chapter of life define me — as someone broken, a victim. Or I could choose to see myself as resilient, adaptable and capable.

Looking back, I can hear the stories I was telling myself — and how reframing those stories and asking questions about the choices available to me helped me shift perspective and move on.

Little did I know back then that my career and passion would take me into the realms of people development and coaching many years later, where I would support others in navigating change, realising they have choices, finding their voice and becoming more visible.

For a second snippet of a story, fast forward to my corporate career. Picture a shiny office in central London. I'm the only woman in a room full of men.

One senior leader rolls his bloodshot eyes at me, expands across the boardroom table, looking remarkably like a walrus and dismisses my detailed change planning as over-engineered. He says we should focus on the financials first — the other things can wait.

I'm stunned. Just beyond that boardroom are real people. Loyal employees, human beings with families. They deserve to understand the changes coming their way. They deserve respect.

But I'm told — again — that the soft, fluffy stuff can wait.

Even now, I remember the tightness in my throat. I scan the room for support, but no one makes eye contact. I'm a lone voice. My emotions rise. My eyes prickle. I silently coach myself to hold it together. I calmly gather my things and leave the room.

I had never walked out of a board meeting before.

In that moment, I didn't have the tools to respond differently — but I do now. And I vowed two things that day.

Firstly, I would never allow someone else's dismissal to silence me again.

And secondly, I would use my voice to honour my values — even in difficult situations.

As women, we often inherit messages that tell us to stay small. Be agreeable, accommodating, likeable and non-disruptive. Keep the peace. Don't rock the boat.

But during change, we're presented with a choice.

To let the challenge diminish us — or to rewrite our inner narrative, examine our limiting assumptions, choose a new story, step into the unknown and be seen. To own our voice — especially when the ground beneath us is shifting. To be boldly visible, even when we feel unsure.

And to embrace the coaching skills that help us do just that.

Consider this.

Being visible during change shows confidence and adaptability. People trust those who show up fully and transparently — even when the path is unclear.

So, ask yourself, "How can you use visibility to create stability during change?"

When we speak up during transitions, we model courage and normalise vulnerability. Our voice gives others permission to show up authentically and do the same.

So, here's another question, "How can your voice offer reassurance or direction during change?"

In uncertainty, it's tempting to play it safe. But staying quiet or small makes us invisible.

Being seen — even when it's uncomfortable — creates influence and impact.

So, what's one small yet bold action you could take during change to remain visible?

Remember, lasting change doesn't come from action alone. It involves knowing who you are and what drives you. So, what's your story?

What part of it are you ready to rewrite? How do you want to show up during change? When everything around you feels uncertain — will you shrink? Or will you rise?

Because when the ground shifts, your voice matters more than ever.

I share my stories not because they're unique — but because they're universal. We've all experienced times of change when we felt unsure, small and invisible. But we don't have to stay there.

Oh, and about the 'walrus in the boardroom'? I got an apology. I was heard. My advice was acted upon. And as a result, my credibility soared.

And now? I use my 30+ years in senior HR roles, combined with 18+ years as a professional coach, to support leaders and teams to navigate change with visibility, voice and choice.

Let's remember.

We all have the power to choose visibility during change.

We all have the power to lead through change.

We all have the power to be seen.

Are you ready to step into it?

Points For Reflection

What experience of change have you overcome and how can you use that strength to be more visible now?

When was the last time you silenced yourself during change? What would it feel like to step forward next time?

What core value do you want to honour more visibly during times of change and how might that shape your choices and actions?

"A girl should be two things — who and what she wants."

Coco Chanel

Meet The Author

Andie Donaldson-Smith is an experienced and authentic leader in the workplace and facilities management industry. Growing up with several mental health conditions, Andie has never allowed others' perceptions of what she may or may not be capable of to slow her down and stop her from achieving her goals. As a neurodiverse black female, she has fought hard for others like herself and has recently stepped into a mentor role. Since 2022, Andie has been on a journey to become a British Sign Language Interpreter as an ally for the deaf community and is currently enrolling for her Level 3 qualification.

Walk Alongside Your Anxiety — Turning Your Inner Demons Into Allies

Andie Donaldson-Smith

Andie confronted her demons, humanised them and got them to work with her instead of against her. Follow her empowering journey to reclaim her power — and find the courage to do the same.

I want to tell you a story.

My story. Your story. Our story.

Let me share how anxiety showed up and messed with my life for years. I'll give you a glimpse into feelings and situations that may feel familiar — and help you reframe how you tackle these too.

In this one short chapter, we're going to figure out how to get those pesky inner demons to behave, to stop tripping us up, stop kicking us in the teeth when we're down and maybe, just maybe, start walking alongside us — for once — as allies.

The cool thing about this approach is that you can take and use it with any inner demon. Honestly, we all have them, don't we? Mine was anxiety.

Sitting on the cold tiled floor of Westfield Shopping Centre, leaning against a vacant storefront, was not how I'd planned my day.

People passing by glanced curiously, inquiringly, but I didn't care at that moment. Anxiety had overwhelmed me and I needed to make myself as small and invisible as possible — this was my coping mechanism. I needed a moment to regroup and ground myself.

This was an old coping mechanism for me — and maybe you have your tried-and-tested ways of dealing with your inner demons too. To give you even more confidence, here are three of my strategies to add to your toolkit.

The battle.

The new plan of attack.

The journey forwards.

First comes the battle. Let me say right off the bat that I'm not a doctor, I'll give you that, nor am I a scientist.

What I have though is powerful. Lived experience that has served me well and may also help you on your empowerment journey.

I've struggled with my mental health and inner demons since I was nine and I've been in and out of hospitals in what seems like a never-ending cycle trying to manage these conditions. You don't need the full details, but for context, I have two personality disorders, depression and an invisible disability. And, of course, anxiety.

So, what is anxiety?

Put simply, it's a b*tch. No two ways about it.

And if you haven't experienced it, let me tell you that it can creep up when you least expect it to and at the same time, it can be a constant state of being.

For me, it made me shake. It brought me to tears without warning. It would grab a limb, pin me down, wrap itself around me and squeeze like a boa constrictor. In short, it was pretty much crippling at times.

Sound familiar?

Let's be honest. What I'm offering is not a chance for you to be cured of your demons. I can't offer miracles — there is no cure. But we can get them to work with us.

I still get palpitations and experience a heightened state of alertness — and the regular state of being overwhelmed penetrates every one of my senses. And when an episode creeps up, it can sometimes still consume me and take a couple of days or more to recover from.

My medication helps, but the anxiety demon is so bloody relentless and will do whatever it can to disrupt my life whenever and wherever. I needed to stop and work out how to tackle this differently.

My new plan of attack began to emerge.

I don't know when it happened, but one day, I sat back, took a moment to reflect and finally humanised my anxiety demon.

In doing so, I found I could converse with her and ask some long-overdue questions.

"Ok, I'm listening now. What the hell do you want?"

"You scream at me regularly. Well, the tables are turning now, madam."

"Are you trying to tell me something, teach me something, protect me from something?"

"When you rear your ugly head, is there a pattern I'm missing?"

Asking these questions allowed for a more productive interaction with my anxiety.

Here's an example of a conversation.

Me — "Why are you always there when I plan to visit a particular friend? You are with me in the lead-up preparations and on the journey. You vibrate through my being when I'm with them and I go home with residual anxiety."

Anxiety — "This friendship has sadly run its course. This isn't a time when I want to show up. I'm just trying to let you know that this situation — and this person — are toxic, and I'll keep showing up until you get the message."

That was a real moment for me in relation to this friendship and it changed everything.

I made adjustments and sadly had to say goodbye. Don't get me wrong — it was hard but needed. I decided to trust my anxiety as she was right. I only had to listen.

And these conversations can work in a multitude of scenarios.

The question — "Anxiety, why are you always present on Friday nights when the weekend is supposed to be a good time?"

Anxiety — "You've planned too much this weekend. Cut something back — you don't have to do it all."

The question — "Why do you make me feel miserable on a Sunday and disrupt my sleep way into the early hours of Monday morning?"

Anxiety — "Your job isn't right for you anymore. You've peaked and need a break, or to work on an exit plan and move into something that brings you joy."

The question — "Why do you start acting up when the in-laws are due?"

Anxiety — "Maybe you need new in-laws? Is that a viable option? Ahem, sorry, but you did ask."

Luckily, I don't have in-laws, but you catch my drift.

It seemed there was a new journey forward, and I was grateful for that.

Who told us we had to fight our inner demons? When did we learn to run away from them or pretend they weren't there? We certainly wouldn't ignore a physical issue such as a bone fracture or a tooth infection.

So, by taking my approach, maybe you can reframe your demons and reach a point where you can identify if they, too, exist to help you.

Unlearn the long-held belief that the demons are a negative part of you. Remove your blinkers, get curious and stop berating yourself.

Get to know your demons as though they are a new friend and if you're hesitant to do this, ask yourself, "What's the worst that could happen?"

Is how you're coping with your demons right now serving you? Or are you ready to accept that they aren't going anywhere, so you may as well embrace them and get them on your side?

Let's end this story at the start of a new chapter. Have those conversations. They are empowering and life changing.

Which path will you take?

Points For Reflection

Spot the signal — think back to a moment when your anxiety (or other demon) showed up loud and proud. Looking at it now with a bit of distance, can you see what it might've been trying to warn you about or protect you from?

Pull up a chair — picture your anxiety as a person sitting next to you. Not an enemy, but someone who's maybe just a bit panicked and confused. What would you say to her if she was your friend? What might she say back? Write the conversation out like a script or dialogue. See how your feelings shift when you stop shouting at her and start talking with her.

Walk with, not against. Ask yourself honestly, "Am I ready to stop dragging my demons behind me and let them walk beside me instead?" If the answer's yes — perhaps even a soft maybe, — what's holding you back from starting now? Close your eyes, visualise putting down the weapons, surrendering the shackles, turning around, giving anxiety your hand, lifting them and taking the next steps together.

"Stop chasing the ideal of a woman
you were not born to be,
and start embracing she
who is fizzing fiercely to be seen
right in front of your eyes."

Donna Ashworth

Meet The Author

Katja Brodt de Sousa has worked as a Fraud Investigation Auditor for three leading global players in the accountancy industry. Her fascination with understanding the unconscious behaviour pattern, often leading to suffering, stress and confusion, ignited her decision to train as a Psychotherapist. For the last 18 years, she has helped clients as a qualified MA Psychotherapist to understand how past experiences shape current relationships and influence decision-making. Her therapeutic work rewires unhealthy connections of thoughts, beliefs, feelings, and behaviours and demystifies relationship patterns. She provides services for adults and couples.

Come Home To Your Truth

Katja Brodt de Sousa

Katja shares her journey through various spiritual practices and how her search for healing from personal and mental health struggles eventually led her to a faith that brought inner peace, lasting transformation and connection.

In December 1982, a classic movie was released called *E.T.* I was nine and identified with this little alien. I, too, wanted to phone home and then 'go home'. I sensed I did not belong here and that there was something more out there to connect to.

It is not only E.T. and me. In 2022, a British study revealed that 49% of participants, which translates to a staggering 26 million people in the UK, reported feeling lonely occasionally, repeatedly or always.[1]

We are in a crisis of belonging and when we feel we don't belong, we experience a mismatch between the quality of relationships we have and those we want. Loneliness results from a lack of belonging — and loneliness at its core means a lack of connection.

I had the privilege of a wonderful connection with the American author Louise Hay while I was on her training programme, *You Can Heal Your Life.* At one point, she took me aside, looked at me with her beautiful piercing blue eyes and said, "My child, let your light shine." This brief yet intimate connection was pivotal for my spiritual healing work journey.

I kicked off my training at the Arthur Findlay College in Stansted. With its impressive Stansted Hall and acres of landscaped grounds, this wonderful historic building quickly became my home for advancing me in spiritualism and psychic sciences. I enhanced my clairvoyance and clairsentient and began communicating with the spirit world.

Around the same time, I attended a wedding at a magical, peaceful place called Taplow Court, where I was introduced to Japanese Nichiren Buddhism. Hearing the members chant the Nam Myoho Renge Kyo mantra in unison felt soothing. I recalled the deeply moving autobiographical movie *'What's Love Got To Do*

With It', Tina Turner's true story about her rise to stardom and leaving her abusive husband. She was a practitioner of Nichiren Buddhism and chanted the same mantra. I was drawn to its philosophy of taking responsibility for self-empowerment and inner transformation, contributing to a better and more peaceful world. The same year, I converted to Buddhism.

In my 30s, I had the honour of being asked to join a wonderful global sisterhood movement. The vision was to work with the universal laws and become female empowerment leaders to consciously align with a higher consciousness (the Source) and promote a more loving reality. We followed the Lightworker process and through our transformational work, we believed we could raise frequencies and help Mother Earth ascend to the 5th dimension (a higher state of spiritual consciousness). Our purpose was to establish peace on Earth and transmute darkness and fear into light, compassion and love.

In addition, I became a certified medium to access The Akashic Records. This is said to be the universal library database that holds records of our soul journeys and purposes. During a reading, with the client's consent, I would retrieve information about their life purpose, past lessons and future possibilities, helping them find answers to their confusion and struggles.

I then explored the world of plant medicine. Despite the lack of scientific evidence to support many of the health claims, I experimented with indigenous shamanic rituals. These included Kambo, a poisonous secretion from the giant monkey frog that is applied to the skin to heal the body and strengthen the immune system; Rape, a finely ground tobacco that is forcefully blown up your nostrils to promote grounding, focus the mind and disrupt ruminating; Ayahuasca, a potent psychedelic brew known to induce altered states of consciousness to give personal insights, a sense of connection and to treat mood disorders; and San Pedro, a bitter cactus flesh consumed for its psychoactive properties and used to heighten awareness, enhance creativity and gain personal insights.

My main goal was to find the ultimate technique to speed up healing and reduce suffering.

During this time, I started a collaboration with three internationally known shamans as their go-to psychotherapist. I was responsible for the aftercare of their participants of shamanic ceremonies to integrate their healing experiences when coming back to the reality of their day-to-day lives or dealing with flashbacks from 'bad trips'.

The above might sound exotic and excessive, but it matches my seeking spirit and curious, inquisitive personality. When I commit to something, I am all in. To this date, I'm fully committed to finding ways to reduce unnecessary human suffering and emotional pain.

And yet, as time passed, I noticed a disturbing and concerning pattern in me.

The highs from these experiences were always short-lived and inevitably followed by a crash — a sense of emptiness, loneliness and sadness. Like E.T., I was still lost. Each low pushed me to seek out the next ritual, ceremony, retreat or training, hoping it would finally bring lasting peace.

Instead of becoming stronger, resilient, empowered and happier, my reality was the opposite. I became hypersensitive and easily overwhelmed by noises, smells, people, places.

I needed longer recovery time from the rituals to function normally and carry out daily tasks such as shopping or cleaning the house. This was confusing. I was working with the most powerful spiritual healing modalities currently on offer, but even this didn't prevent my diagnosis of anxiety, depression and fatigue.

I heard this quote from the Buddhist spiritual leader, His Holiness the Dalai Lama. "There are many different religions and cultures in the world, and each has developed to suit its people. Because of that, I always recommend that it's best to keep the religion you were born into and not to mix them."[2]

Could that be true? Did I bring my mental health struggle on myself by practising Spiritualism, Mediumship, Buddhism, New Age and Shamanism? Did I simply meddle and combine too many different things?

In this reflection, I found the truth. One truth was that the religion I was born into was Christianity. Until then, it did not resonate with me and never sparked any interest. To put it frankly, I found church boring and its teachings unexciting. It just never connected with me.

Another truth was that anything that contributes to anxiety, panic attacks, depression, stress and confusion is not empowering.

Pondering the idea of 'truth', I recalled a passage from my confirmation ceremony. Each teenager had been given a Bible verse — mine from John 8:32 — "Then you will know the truth, and the truth will set you free."

I paused.

I stopped practising everything I believed in. I gave myself space to understand the scripture. And true to my personality, I was fully committed. I wanted to know. I needed to know. I dedicated myself to reading the Bible for at least one hour a day. If anyone had told me this would lead to my most profound and positive transformative experience, I would have laughed it off.

Now, I am deeply grateful to share my story. Six years ago, I surrendered my life to Jesus Christ, accepting Him as my Lord and Saviour instead of trying to save the world myself. In doing so, I found a genuine connection to myself, others and God.

Since then, I've experienced lasting peace, calmness and a loving, supportive connection with my family and friends. For the past five years, I've lived free from anxiety, depression and dark thoughts. This starkly contrasted with what was happening in the outside world during the Covid lockdown — a time marked by fear and isolation while I felt a deep inner sense of peace, joy and connection.

Looking back, I am grateful I recognised that certain choices, no matter how positive they seem, how promising they sound or how beneficial they have been for others, if the long-term consequences are affecting you negatively in body, mind and spirit, keeping you insanely busy and financially stretched, it is not worth exploring.

My truth and faith have set me free and I now understand that faith can take many forms. For me, it came through discovering the scripture and I can humbly confirm that the verse from John 8:32 became my reality.

This is only my unique experience — one woman, one story. And like E.T., I found my home, roots and sense of empowerment.

We each have a different story with our own challenges. I truly hope and wish, paraphrasing John 8:32, that you too can find your truth and the truth will set you free.

Points For Reflection

Regularly take a mental and emotional inventory of the practices you call spiritual.

Ask yourself if they are helping you feel calm, centred, stable and connected. Or are they making you feel anxious, low and overwhelmed?

Find a group or an individual that shares your values and interests. Forming strong relationships can help eliminate loneliness by providing support and a sense of belonging.

Meet The Author

Karen Farrell is a Breathwork Expert, Coach and Speaker who empowers women to break through limitations and step into their full potential by tapping into their most powerful resource — their breath! With a Bachelor of Music and a background as a trained singer, Karen has experienced first-hand the transformative power of effective breathing techniques. Her journey in music taught her the importance of breath control, which has been invaluable in building resilience and navigating life's highs and lows. Through her coaching, Karen helps others reconnect with their breath to quiet self-doubt, build inner confidence and rise into a more empowered version of themselves.

How To Breathe Your Way Through Fear And Rise

Karen Farrell

In this chapter, Karen describes the power of breathing through the inevitable fears and doubts that life throws at us and how your breath is your secret empowering weapon.

"I almost forgot to breathe."

I remember the first time I saw this review stretched across a giant movie poster advertising a horror film called *See No Evil*. The review implied that the people involved were so scared they almost forgot to breathe. As I stood there looking at the poster, I paused and thought about how often fear grips us in everyday moments. How often do we forget to breathe, not because of a horror film, but because of fear?

I'm not necessarily talking about the jump-scare, creepy-soundtrack kind of fear, but the real, everyday kind. The kind that shows up quietly and whispers, "What if you fail?" or "Who do you think you are?" or "What if they say no?" The fear that creeps in and paralyses you. That type of fear.

You see, fear is probably the number one thing that keeps us stuck. That stops us from rising and becoming the best version of ourselves. And if there's one thing I've learned, it's this —your breath is your secret weapon when it comes to overcoming fear. And when you learn to use it — and I mean really use it, everything shifts.

Before we go any further, I want to share three fascinating things I've learned about fear over the past few years. Some of them you might already know and some might surprise you.

The first point is that we, as humans, are only born with two fears. That's right — just two. These are fear of falling and fear of loud noises. So, if we're only born with two fears, then all those other fears, fear of regret, fear of failure, fear of judgment, fear of success — they are learned. They are imagined. They are just created in our minds. Stories we've picked up from childhood, experiences and the world around us. Stories that repeat in our heads until we believe them. But here's the good news. If we can learn fear, we can also unlearn it.

The second point is that faith and fear are the same thing. Sounds crazy, right? But if you think about it, faith and fear require you to believe in something you cannot see. Fear is believing in the worst-case scenario and faith is believing in the best-case scenario. Fear says, "This will go wrong." Faith says, "This will grow you." So, if we're going to believe in the invisible anyway, why not choose the version that empowers you? Why not choose faith? Why not choose you?

Finally, the third point is that 'fear is excitement without breath'. I'll never forget the moment I read this intriguing statement in the book *The Big Leap* by American psychologist Gay Hendricks.[1] The author believes that this is one of the greatest pieces of wisdom he's ever heard from Dr Fritz Perls, a psychiatrist and the founder of Gestalt Therapy and I have to agree with him. Gay Hendricks explains that "The very same mechanisms that produce excitement also produce fear and any fear can be transformed into excitement by breathing fully with it."

When you think about it, fear and excitement are two sides of the same coin. They feel almost identical in our bodies — our hearts race, our palms sweat and we feel that rush of adrenaline.

But there's one key difference — excitement happens when you're breathing and fear happens when you're not.

Think about it. Every time you've been paralysed by fear — whether stepping onto a stage, having a tough conversation, or trying something new — you've probably held your breath. It's your body's automatic response to danger. But here's the thing — the danger isn't real most of the time. It's just a story we've created in our minds. And the way to break free from that story, to move from fear to excitement, from doubt to action, from nerves to progress, is simple. You must breathe. Because the less breath you feed your fear, the bigger your fear gets.

There's one sport that shows just how powerful breathwork can be. If you've never heard of freediving, it's this incredible, slightly insane sport where people dive hundreds of feet underwater on a single breath. No oxygen tank. No gear. No mouthpiece. Just their bodies, their lungs and their minds.

Freedivers have incredible mental, physical and emotional wellbeing because they can control their breath. Most people assume that when it comes to freediving, it's about holding the breath for as long as possible, but here's the thing — the trick isn't holding the breath. It's controlling it before the dive. If freedivers let their mind spiral into fear, they'd never make it. But when they slow their breath, they slow their heart rate and suddenly find a reserve of strength that makes it possible to stay underwater for so long.

We can use this technique, too. When we pause, slow down and tune into our breath, we tap into this incredible inner power — a power that helps us face our fears, silence doubts and take that big, bold, scary action.

Now, we might not be diving to the bottom of the ocean every day, but I bet you've faced moments in your life where fear has held you back. Maybe it's asking for a promotion, starting your own business, writing that book, or just saying yes to something that terrifies you.

In those moments, your mind is going to tell you, "You can't do this," "It's too big," "It's too scary." And that fear will tighten your chest and make you feel stuck. But here's the truth — you're not stuck. You're just not breathing!

I'd like to share a simple breathing technique I use to overcome my fears and doubts. It's backed by science and beautifully simple to do. It's called the Physiological Sigh. The term was coined by scientists in the 1930s and has recently been popularised by Andrew Huberman, an American neuroscientist, who believes it's one of the best breathing tools for stress reduction.[2]

Here's how it works.

Take a long, slow inhale through your nose, filling your lungs with air. Immediately follow the first inhale with a second, shorter breath, ensuring you're taking in a little more air. Then exhale slowly and audibly through your mouth like a sigh.

It feels so good, doesn't it?

This simple breathing pattern signals to your nervous system that you're safe. It slows your heart rate. It clears your mind. It shifts you from panic into peace. And when your body knows you're safe, your courage returns.

This isn't magic — this is science. Your breath is directly connected to your brain. When you're stressed or afraid, your breathing becomes shallow and fast. This signals to your brain that you're in danger, even if the 'threat' is just a passive-aggressive email from a colleague, a presentation you need to deliver, or a tough conversation you must have with someone. However, you send the opposite message when you consciously slow your breathing using techniques like the Physiological Sigh. And suddenly, you can think again. The thing that felt so overwhelming now feels manageable. Suddenly, you feel totally in control.

I truly believe that your breath is your most powerful resource because when you control your breath, you control your thoughts and when you control your thoughts, you control your actions.

So, the next time fear creeps in — and it will — I want you to remember this. Fear is just excitement without the breath — and you have the power to turn that fear into excitement simply by breathing through it. And when you do, you'll never find yourself so scared you forget to breathe, like they did in the horror movie.

So, breathe.

Breathe through the doubt. Breathe through the fear. Breathe through the scariest moments and you'll find a power inside you that nothing can stop.

Because when you master your breath, you master your life.

And that is when you rise.

Points For Reflection

Think back to a recent moment when fear made you freeze or hold your breath. What would it have felt like to pause, breathe deeply and take one small action step forward?

What would it look like to choose faith over fear today?

If fear wasn't an option, what would you do?

"There is no limit to what we, as women, can accomplish."

Michelle Obama

Meet The Author

Kier Adair is an International Brand Photographer, Visual Strategist, Speaker and best-selling author, passionate about empowering ambitious women to have the confidence to be seen for their superpowers. She is an expert in visual branding after 20+ years in marketing at Marks & Spencer, including time in the international group, heading up Visual Merchandising across Central Europe. Kier enables others to thrive with her unique approach and experience, blending her passion for lifestyle photography with her knowledge of connecting and converting through her visual expertise. As Founder of The Speak and Shine Collection, she not only takes women from unseen, but unheard to unstoppable too.

Finding Joy Through My Lens

Kier Adair

In this inspiring chapter, Kier shares her story of rediscovering her joy after many years of chasing the wrong version of success. See how following her passion and purpose made a much bigger impact than she ever imagined.

Photography was my go-to. My escape from reality. My source of pure joy. It fuelled my thirst for travel and adventure, always with my camera in hand. It allowed me to see a whole new perspective — the extraordinary in the everyday.

But my passion got tabled as a hobby I could always return to. I was compelled to pursue my academic qualifications and corporate career for 'true success'. How could photography possibly be a serious career? Where would I even begin to turn my passion into purpose? Why should I get to follow my heart? I didn't have the belief or see that path for me.

Or did I? When I stopped and took time to see, life presented some very different options. Could I make it work? Would I even dare to dream?

Let me take you back several years. I'm 19 and at the airport for the first time ever with my camera, notebook and pack on my back. I'm about to embark on the journey of my life with a round-the-world ticket in my hand, pure excitement in my heart and my spirited inner child leading my head. Little did I know I was about to start a new chapter. One of being fearless, free and full of wanderlust. One that was truly me living my best life. One that I would keep coming back to years later in my search for the real me I had lost along the way.

On my travels, it was just my camera and me. I was in my element, curious and excited about what could be. Always exploring off the beaten track and climbing the highest spot — often at three in the morning to catch the sunrise. Always going that extra mile and doing what others wouldn't to get THAT shot. It was the first time strangers had said, "You really could make something of your photography." But I wasn't ready to listen.

In those days without the Internet or mobile phones, it was a tour of self-discovery. Travelling alone, connecting with others was the only way to make things happen and make the most of every day. I learnt so many powerful lessons — especially the art of building relationships and the importance of being around inspiring people.

This gap year ignited a fire in me. But when I returned home, I was at a crossroads. It was my 'sliding doors' moment. I was meant to fulfil my desire to pursue photography at some point — just not yet. I chose the traditional route mapped out for me over my creative passion. It was the safe bet. The path that matched my own and society's expectations.

I now know there were signs at every station. Taking the summers to travel the world. Studying for my dissertation in the Costa Rican Rain Forest. Deferring another year after university to take an overland truck across Africa. All incredible experiences, photographing amazing people and places, but still, I thought it was time to take life 'seriously'. Time to take that 'proper job' that was waiting for me. Time to accept that whilst I was a talented photographer, it wasn't a real option.

I still remember the first day of my corporate life. Dressed like Lady Di, in a beige suit, fancy neck scarf and killer high heels. I thought, "What am

I doing?" Ten days before, I'd been in the African bush, enjoying nature, mostly barefoot and, yes, peeing in said bush.

But I was incredibly ambitious. I'd earned a place on the coveted graduate programme at Marks & Spencer — an opportunity others would have given anything for. Back then, I thought success meant status and salary. I thought the higher I climbed the corporate ladder, the more successful I would be. So that's what I did.

I carved out a creative role in M&S and loved what I did — heading up visual merchandising across Central Europe, living in Prague, and looking like I had it all. Yet, I always felt like a square peg in a round hole (or, in my case, a Pentax in a sea of Nikons!). I felt boxed in with everything clipped. Even my international travel, although incredible, was on someone else's agenda. It was all for someone else — and I was not living in my truth.

Only when I had my daughter and during my maternity year did I get a glimpse of that 19-year-old again. I'd lost sight of her. I'd lost sight of the freedom I loved and the sense of what I wanted. I began to realise I was chasing the wrong version of success.

Returning to work, I was soon back on the hamster wheel, running to stand still, only this time with the added dimension of 'Mum guilt'. I found myself in yet another lengthy restructure. In the past, during all the numerous redundancy situations, I had seen opportunity. But this time felt very different. The day I heard my job was safe, I cried.

That was the pivotal moment I knew I had to find my joy again. Stop hiding behind a corporate brand and being someone I wasn't. After 22 years of all I'd ever known, aged 45 with a three-year-old, I said goodbye to corporate life. Finally, I could stretch my wings and fly.

I created a portfolio business in visual consulting, property and health and wellness. It led me to personal development and a shift in mindset — from employee to entrepreneur. It gave me the freedom I sought but not the fulfilment. Sensing my frustration, my business coach asked me a simple but powerful question that took me right back to that 19-year-old. Me, my camera and the joy of capturing life.

"What did you always want to do, Kier?"

"Photography," I instantly replied.

"Why aren't you doing that then?"

It was like she had flicked a switch.

This was when I discovered brand photography, something I didn't even know existed. I couldn't believe it! Other photography genres had never felt right for me. Too boxed in. Too studio based. Too restricted by other people's rules. But this? This was the perfect marriage of my passion for lifestyle imagery and my years in branding, marketing and customer journey. All those years in corporate finally made sense.

Finally, I'd found my purpose.

Of course, it didn't happen overnight. The many reasons for not following my heart earlier took time to overcome.

That 'not good enough' voice — "Why would anyone pay for something that feels easy and fun?"

That 'not trained or qualified' fear — "Why would anyone trust just me and my intuition?"

That 'not a clue where to start' block — well, I just needed to start.

Then came my Eureka moment — not in the bath but in the shower. The penny dropped

— people booked me for how I made them feel, not just for my beautiful images. My intuitive approach, without all the tech, equipment and photography degrees, was my selling point. My strength. My point of difference.

I began to acknowledge my innate superpowers that were so obvious to me, that I hadn't valued before, as well as the power of my experience. Ironically, having left my job to unlock me, I hid my career for several years, thinking it was part of the 'old' me in the corporate box. It was then pointed out that this was also my USP. It was where I had earned my stripes and built my authority.

My business became so much more than me following my heart — it became a way for others to realise their dreams. It became so much bigger than me when I allowed myself to see the impact and ripple effect I could create. That showing up meant those needing to see me did. Brand photography became my reason to be visible. To be the beacon in the lighthouse for others caught in the choppy waters, as I had once been.

When you lean into your passion and joy, life becomes easier, more fulfilling and, yes, so much more fun. Of course, running a business is still challenging and you must be open to constant evolution. With new levels, there are always new devils, but there's always a way forward. When your mission is fuelled by something you love, it never feels like work.

And it doesn't have to stop there. I thought my journey was all about taking people from unseen to unstoppable through brand photography. Now I see it goes beyond that. Founding the Speak and Shine Collection has catapulted me to a new level, championing others to move from unheard to unstoppable, too.

And who knows what's next?

Leaning into my joy has brought me to where I am today. When I was stuck, I returned to that fearless 19-year-old with the round-the-world ticket in my hand and a fire in my belly, knowing if I don't ask, I don't get. If I don't have a voice and be seen, I will never reach my destination, let alone relish the ride. There is nothing more empowering than owning your voice and knowing your purpose.

Enjoy your ride!

Points For Reflection

Trust your intuition and lean into your joy. You don't have to have it all mapped out. Just take the first step.

Invest in yourself and mentors who will challenge your thinking and ask the difficult questions. To see what you don't see, which is often right in front of you.

Stay inquisitive. Surround yourself with vibrant people who ignite you to be more, do more and have more.

Meet The Author

Ann Marie Cunningham is a trusted and awarded expert who works globally with high-profile clients, C-suite executives, and those seeking deeper meaning and purpose. Known for her sharp intuition and dynamic presence, she is a trailblazer in blending coaching and psychotherapy to achieve healing, transformation and growth. Partnering with her clients, Ann Marie fosters compassion and authentic growth by harnessing neuroplasticity to rewire limiting beliefs, reshape thought patterns and develop healthier emotional responses. Her unique approach combines storytelling and therapeutic coaching with creative visualisation, engaging the senses to foster deeper connection and insight.

Storytelling With Purpose

Ann Marie Cunningham

In this deeply personal chapter, Ann Marie invites you to explore the complexities of loss and the pain of the untold story, encouraging you to reflect on yours. She offers a space for deep introspection and the opportunity to rewrite your narrative with intention and compassion.

When I lost my youngest sister, Una, in 2004, something inside me shattered. It wasn't just the pain of her passing, it was the trauma that wouldn't leave. That trauma became a shadow that followed me, lingering in every part of my life. Maybe, just like me, you've carried trauma that feels heavy, unresolved and always present, subtly shaping the way you live.

I was preparing the Easter egg hunt for my three children, arranging the little signs that read 'The Easter Bunny Went This Way' when an unfamiliar voice on the phone shared the devastating news. "The ambulance crew admitted her with a ruptured brain aneurysm." As I sat beside Una, my body carried the heartbeat of new life. I was 37 weeks pregnant with my fourth child.

I spent weeks with Una as she lay in a coma in the high-dependency unit, listening to the relentless beeping of the life support machines. The rhythm became a strange comfort, a reminder that she was still with me, her breath, shallow and steady, synchronised with the beeps. And then the beeping stopped. And in that silence, I heard something deeper.

In *Stillness Speaks,* Eckhart Tolle says, “Silence is more than the absence of noise. It is intelligence itself, the unconditioned consciousness underlying all form.”[1]

It was not only an ending. It was an invitation, a calling into something unknown.

Years passed before my understanding of *Stillness Speaks* emerged.

I don’t know if you’ve ever experienced the feeling when something so constant or present suddenly disappears. It wasn’t just the silence. It was the visceral response in my body when that rhythm stopped. I’d hear it in my head when I was driving. I’d hear it when I was asleep. And when it wasn’t there, the absence was overwhelming. I would hold my breath and freeze.

The heartbeat of my newborn was a stark contrast to the silence that followed Una's passing. I was familiar with the pattern of life and death, having lost my father when my firstborn was just six months old and losing a younger sister when my secondborn was only nine weeks old. Each loss came during a time of profound personal change, birth and death so closely intertwined.

Trauma cannot be processed in the mind — it lives in the body. In *The Body Keeps the Score*, Bessel van der Kolk explains that trauma is stored in our tissues, affecting how we experience life.[2] It becomes a physiological imprint that influences our emotions and actions. Gabor Maté echoes this in his book, *The Myth of Normal: Trauma, Illness, and Healing in a Toxic Culture,* stating that trauma is the emotional pain we internalise when it can't be expressed.[3]

Dissociation is the sense of being disconnected from yourself. It becomes the body's survival mechanism when emotional pain becomes overwhelming. This is why many of us live with numbness, a sense of being disconnected from our lives. This dissociation pulls us away from who we are, from the joy and life inside us.

Healing requires becoming aware of how trauma is held within our bodies, understanding its impact and releasing it through compassionate self-awareness and integration.

In the aftermath of Una's death, I found myself unable to return to the life I had before. My identity had shifted, my drive for success diminished and my passion for providing tech solutions was dead. In time, I engaged with deep introspection to seek understanding and I transitioned from my established technology business to the world of psychology, psychotherapy and neuroscience. I had a desire to understand the human experience more deeply, how trauma, loss and emotional pain shape us and how to heal from them.

And as I moved into this new identity, this new purpose, I began to recognise something profound — post-traumatic growth. This was the transformation that came from reflecting on the past with curiosity, with a deep fascination to understand it and derive new meaning from it. It was about transforming it into something meaningful.

Yet even with all the education, the work I did and the growth I experienced, I didn't realise that my trauma wasn't truly processed. It stayed buried, tied to something much earlier in my life. I didn't understand why it had been so challenging to move forward after Una's passing until years later, when I found the root cause of my trauma.

More than 40 years after leaving school, I sat in my garden reading Vicky Phelan's memoir, *Overcoming* and everything came rushing back.[4] In her story, Phelan describes surviving a car crash she was in at 15 — the smells, the sounds, the eerie silence. And suddenly, out of nowhere, I screamed the name of my childhood friend, Carmel, who had died in a car accident at 15.

I was working a summer job at the time and it was considered best that I didn't take time off for Carmel's funeral. I never got to say goodbye to her. I never returned to school. I never saw my classmates again. I worked in that cigar-making factory for three years, an adult world separated from my teenage life.

I became aware of the deep connection between my trauma and the unprocessed pain of losing Carmel. This awakening shifted everything for me. These losses, these moments of trauma, shape our identity through the relational, systemic and transformational forces that influence who we become.

Adolescence is a critical period for identity formation. It's when we begin to shape our sense of self and it's done in large part through relationships with others, especially peers. During this time, these relationships provide emotional support, challenge and a mirror of who we are becoming. The people around us help shape our beliefs, values and place in the world.

The bonds we form during adolescence become foundational for navigating the world as adults. The problem is when these relationships are interrupted, stunted or isolated, as in my case, the process of identity formation becomes incomplete. I missed the critical emotional support that could have helped me process the trauma of losing Carmel. Instead, I was left to carry it alone.

In adolescence, we need to connect with others to build emotional resilience and develop a stable sense of self. I didn't have that. Instead, I was disconnected from my peers, working through trauma without the space or language to process it. The absence of these vital relationships left a wound I carried for years.

To truly understand my buried trauma and heal the root cause, I needed to delve deeper and this required specialist trauma work. I had to go beyond the surface and start working with my subconscious mind, where deeply held limiting beliefs shaped how I viewed myself and the world around me. I needed to reclaim my sense of self, which required harnessing the power of neuroplasticity through creating new meaning and new neural pathways.

Empowering beliefs are the birthright of every human being.

I am enough. I am worthy. I belong.

These beliefs are universal truths. They apply to everyone.

What about you? What limiting beliefs might you be holding about yourself? Do you ever question where these beliefs come from? Are they yours, or are they beliefs passed down from previous generations? Maybe they're cultural beliefs or societal pressures you've absorbed over time.

It's not always easy to let go of long-held beliefs, yet reclaiming your birthright to believe you are enough, that you are worthy and that you belong can be a powerful step in your healing journey. By shifting your beliefs, you're not only transforming how you see yourself. You're changing how you show up in the world, live, and empower yourself to rise.

I am always mindful of the beautiful Maya Angelou quote from *I Know Why The Caged Bird Sings* — 'There is no greater agony than bearing an untold story inside you.'[5] I gently encourage you to tell your story and share your voice.

It's my privilege to witness the paradox of pain and healing in my work. I recognise that my ability to hold space with compassion and respect emerged during the most painful time of my life, sitting beside my sister in a coma. It was in that space I learned the true power of presence. And you can, too.

Points For Reflection

What untold story lies within you? What does it feel like?

Trauma and adverse childhood experiences leave imprints on us. How have those imprints shaped who you are today? What would it look like to transform them with purpose?

When you think about your past, what strength have you gained from facing what was hard? How can you use that strength now to move forward?

Meet The Author

Debbie Hancock is a Chartered Management Accountant, Certified Financial Coach and experienced Finance Director. With a background in senior finance roles and a deep understanding of business strategy, she now combines her expertise with coaching to empower individuals to build financial confidence and joy. Debbie is passionate about helping people rewrite their money stories and create a life of freedom on their own terms. Her insights have been featured in *The Times*, *The Metro* and *Authority Magazine*, and she speaks regularly about financial wellbeing and empowerment. She believes that with the right support, anyone can be good with money.

Anyone Can Be Good With Money

Debbie Hancock

In this chapter, Debbie shares personal insights to help you rewrite your money story and build financial confidence because, with the right tools and support, anyone can be good with money.

It's time to challenge the myth that only certain people are 'good with money.'

Too often, we're taught that money is only for those with an innate skill or ability to manage it, but this couldn't be further from the truth.

I want to show you that anyone can be good with money, and I mean anyone. It doesn't matter where you're starting from or what your past looks like. The key lies in understanding your money story, recognising any beliefs holding you back, and being open to rewriting the narrative you've lived with for so long.

Money isn't just about numbers. It's about freedom, choices and the life you want to create. It's deeply personal and often shaped by stories we've inherited without realising it. These stories affect how we view money, how we use it and how we relate to it on a deeper level.

When we change how we think about money, we change everything. Our bank accounts, relationships, confidence and, most importantly, the life we're building. That's where true financial confidence starts, not with budgets, spreadsheets, or rules, but with understanding and embracing the deeper stories that shape our reality.

I was told I was good with money for most of my life. I was the responsible one, the planner, the saver, the person who always knew how to stretch every penny. I thought I would be safe if I could stick to a tight budget, avoid debt and keep a rainy-day fund.

But here's the truth I eventually discovered. My version of being good with money wasn't about managing numbers. It was about control.

Underneath the surface, my relationship with money wasn't rooted in freedom or joy. It was rooted in fear. I was afraid of not having enough. I was scared of not being safe. And honestly, I was fearful of letting go.

But real financial wellbeing isn't just about control. It's about ease, enjoyment and emotional freedom. It's about using money as a tool to create a life you love.

What I discovered through my financial coaching qualification changed everything. I realised that financial freedom begins not with numbers but with stories. Our stories. And the good news? Anyone can be good with money. You just need to believe it's possible and begin.

Growing up, money was tight. From a young age, I learned to budget, save and make do. I thought if I kept a firm grip, I'd be safe.

For a long time, I believed that narrative. After all, it worked — for a while. I had my emergency fund. I made responsible choices. But what I didn't see was that beneath the surface, my relationship with money was rooted in fear and lack.

Money had become my security blanket. I held onto it so tightly, afraid that letting go would leave me vulnerable. I thought I was protecting myself, but in fact, I was keeping myself stuck.

True financial wellbeing goes beyond control. It's about allowing money to enhance our lives.

It's about using it in alignment with our values, our goals and, yes, even our joy.

When I trained as a financial coach, I thought I already had a healthy mindset around money. But the deeper I went, the more I uncovered stories and beliefs that were holding me back.

"If I ask for more, someone else will have less."

"If I buy something just because I want it, that's greedy."

"If I earn too much, I'll lose who I am. I'm that working-class girl."

These thoughts weren't financial facts. They were emotional echoes from my childhood, passed down by well-meaning adults doing their best. But they were no longer serving me.

We all grow up absorbing messages about money, some subtle, some in your face. By the age of seven, our money beliefs are largely set. We all know the sayings, don't we?

"Money doesn't grow on trees."

"The love of money is the root of all evil."

"You have to work hard to make money."

These become the soundtrack in our heads, shaping how we view, earn and spend money throughout our lives.

But here's the truth – just because you learned something early in life doesn't mean you have to keep believing it.

Instead, it's about shifting from control to freedom.

One of my favourite movies is *Ratatouille.* There's a line I love, "Anyone can cook." It's a great reminder that anyone can become good at something they once thought was out of reach with the right guidance, practice and willingness to change.

This idea applies to money too.

Maybe you've struggled with numbers. Maybe you've made mistakes. Maybe you've felt shame or regret about past financial decisions. But that doesn't have to be your story forever. You have the power to rewrite it.

You can be the one who breaks free from fear and lack of thinking. You can be the one who looks at money with a new perspective and opens up choices, opportunities and the possibility for more.

And in doing so, you change not only your future but also the future for generations to come. How empowering and exciting is that?

Because money isn't just about accumulation, it's about choice. It's about freedom. It's about saying yes to the things that light you up and no to those that don't.

It's taking your family on holiday, investing in your business, leaving a job that drains you, supporting a loved one or buying a little luxury just because it makes you smile.

That's what I want for everyone — to feel joy around money.

Everything shifted after doing the inner work and experiencing financial coaching for myself. I started choosing meals I wanted when dining out, not just the cheapest option. I let money flow instead of trying to control it.

And I've seen this transformation in my clients, too. People from all walks of life, affluent or not, who've been carrying beliefs that limit their ability to enjoy money. Because it's not about how much you have but how you relate to it.

The practical tools, budgets, spreadsheets and savings pots are helpful. But they're not the whole picture.

Because knowledge alone doesn't change lives.

If knowledge were the answer, we'd all be sorted. There's no shortage of free information online. But transformation doesn't just come from knowing more. It comes from understanding your stories, challenging your beliefs and taking empowered action.

As the saying goes, 'success leaves clues.' So do money stories.

What comes to mind if I ask you to finish this sentence, — "Money is...?" Don't overthink it. Just notice the words. These automatic responses are clues to your beliefs. And your beliefs shape your financial reality.

So many of us carry inherited stories without realising it.

"I'm not good with numbers."

"I've always been bad with money."

"I don't understand finances."

But these stories can be changed. You've already done hard things in life. This is just another one to tackle. And you don't have to do it alone.

I once supported someone close to me who nearly made a life-altering financial decision out of fear. They didn't want to talk about it, but they did. That moment of bravery changed everything. They faced reality and, in doing so, secured their independence.

Can you be brave? Brave enough to look at your bank account. Brave enough to raise your prices. Brave enough to say, "I want more."

Being good with money isn't about being perfect. It's about being intentional. About deciding to take back control in a way that serves you, not out of fear, but from a place of power.

So, let's rewrite your money story.

Let's choose a new narrative rooted in possibility, freedom and joy. One that aligns with your values and your vision for life.

As Remy in *Ratatouille* says, "Change is nature. The part we can influence. And it starts when we decide."

So, let's decide.

And when you do, you won't just change your life. You'll change the future for generations to come.

Points For Reflection

What is the first word that comes to mind when you think about money? Write it down. Don't analyse it because this is a clue to your money story.

What money beliefs did you inherit from your parents or caregivers? Are they still serving you, or is it time to let them go?

What practical step can you take today to move closer to financial freedom? It could be checking your bank account, having an honest conversation, or simply writing down your financial goals.

Meet The Author

Rebecca Leppard is an Indonesian Entrepreneur who ditched her cosy corporate corner office for the dynamic world of tech and consulting in the UK. When the 2020 pandemic forced her to start from scratch in England, she turned hundreds of job rejections into fuel, founding Upgrading Women — a media company helping ambitious women build knockout personal brands. Now a trusted Fractional CMO for seed to Series A startups, Rebecca delivers razor-sharp marketing strategies across luxury hospitality, fintech and tradetech. Between juggling life as a mum of three, she leads a thriving community of global careerwomen building their own ladder to the top.

Personal Branding As A Feminist Move — How Visibility Becomes Resistance In The Era Of Algorithmic Misogyny

Rebecca Leppard

In this chapter, Rebecca shares the grim reality of living in a toxic and violent society and encourages women to show themselves more so they can balance power and influence.

"Rebecca, I thought you were a feminist — why so much make-up?"

"Why do you wear pink all the time?"

"Is that really your branding?"

These questions from neighbours, friends and even my university professor aren't really about aesthetics — they're about fitting into a box. Boxes that only exist because of the unspoken rulebook, which states that serious women dress in neutrals, that feminism should be austere (anyone wanna burn their bra?) and that expertise must be packaged in masculine-coded professionalism.

For generations, women have obediently followed the patriarchy's prescribed path. We've muted our colours, modulated our voices and meticulously groomed ourselves to fit into spaces that were never truly ours in the first place. And like countless migrant women before me, I believed professional success would follow if I played by the rules.

But years of being forced to fit in those spaces have left us unsure of our standing in overtly masculine offices, meetings and boardrooms. We use cognitive disclaimers to avoid disbelief or suspicions of poor judgment when pressed. We hedge with phrases like, "I could be wrong, but..." or "I hope that makes sense?" according to *The Gender Communication Handbook: Conquering Conversational Collisions Between Men and Women*.[1]

But where has being so compliant gotten us?

To answer that question, we need to look no further than our backyards.

My daughter may be conditioned to be more traditional than my mother was in the 80s. In 2023, #TradWife content amassed billions of views, with platforms pushing traditional values to young audiences.[2] This isn't just about Instagram aesthetics — it's algorithmic radicalisation. Scroll through the hashtags and you'll find picture-perfect Victoria sponges captioned with messages like 'A woman's place is in the home' or 'Trying to be a man is a waste of a woman.'

For too long, we've thought that repression of women is only a problem in conflict-ridden poor countries. Sure, we are still allowed to sing and go to school, unlike our sisters in Afghanistan, but statistics paint a horrifying picture of the Western world, too. Out of 50 US states, child marriage remains legal in 37.[3] Meanwhile, in the UK, a mother received 28 months' imprisonment for a late-term abortion in 2023[4] while Victims Commissioner data showed that only 5% of reported rapes resulted in charges that same year.[5]

On top of this, more than 50,000 women and girls were killed by intimate partners or family members in 2023 globally, according to data from the United Nations Office on Drugs and Crime.[6]

The digital landscape is also often alarmingly aggressive now. Recent polling by Amnesty International UK revealed disturbing trends.[7]

That 73% of Gen Z social media users witness misogynistic content online, with half encountering it weekly.

That 53% receive inappropriate emojis on posts and photos.

And that Gen Z women from ethnic minority backgrounds experience significantly higher rates of hate speech than their white counterparts.

You see, the ‘broligarchs’— those hyper-masculine influencers who’ve mastered personal branding to dominate attention — flourish. With 61% of Gen Z attributing the rise in misogynistic language online to statements by political leaders and figures like Andrew Tate (who allegedly has amassed 220,000+ active members in his Hustler University),[8] we’re witnessing systematic oppression through social media. And the trends are rampant here in the UK. The Guardian recently reported on teachers facing students who are overtly influenced by Tate and Trump, who spout racist, homophobic, transphobic and sexist comments in every conversation and don’t believe there will be consequences.[9]

So, what do we do in this new manosphere?

In all our visibility work, we must build strong personal branding as calculated acts of micro rebellion. After all, algorithmic processes on TikTok and other social media sites target vulnerabilities such as loneliness or feelings of loss of control by gamifying harmful content, according to University College London Information Studies.[10] And all in the name of entertainment.

But let's reframe it. This means that we can turn the system on its head. These same algorithms, which were weaponised against us, can become our greatest allies. What if young people micro-dose on topics such as social justice, good habits, mental health and acts of kindness? This is not a rhetorical question — we must dilute toxic content by creating more positive, optimistic, empathetic content ourselves. So, let's revolt by seeing what works in this digital manosphere.

Let me share what I've learned from hard data and harsh experiences.

Share your life online, not as carefully curated lessons or dramatic turning points but simply as they are. No profound wisdom, no 'everything happens for a reason' platitudes. Just authentic experiences — "Well, that didn't go as planned. Moving on to the next one."

The responses to this sort of content have been refreshing for me. Women acknowledge that this is what a typical business day looks like. Some days you win, some days you don't and that's perfectly fine. While we're envying someone's LinkedIn update about their new leadership role, someone else is looking at our small wins with the same awe.

The Oxford Internet Institute found from 168 countries that Internet use is consistently associated with positive well-being. Let's take advantage of having access to influence others. Be everywhere and be useful.[11]

When I first started mentoring other women, particularly those facing multiple marginalisations (neurodivergent, immigrant, women of colour) like myself, I worried I didn't have enough experience to offer. But I've learned that every woman who makes it through a door is responsible for holding it open for others. Don't be the world's best-kept secret, as that's not helpful to anyone, let alone other women.

If you've been wondering what I have personally done in my day-to-day to chip away at the patriarchy one selfie at a time, below is my ritual. This 42-year-old brown woman landed in London in 2020 with her husband and their three children amidst COVID carnage. The script written for her read, 'Stay small. Be grateful. Don't make noise'. But she said no and took the following actions instead.

Every day, I write and post something. It can be short or long. It can be audio, text or video. I just trained my muscles and loosened my nerves. I don't go to the gym, but writing and posting take the same regularity and discipline as physical training to get the most out of them.

Each week, I teach and live by my social media algorithm. I unfollow and remove suggested posts about anything that brings me anxiety, fear and pessimism. I follow accounts that bring me laughter (you should see my meme collection!), inspiration (from fashion to business ideas) and which teach me about history, culture and the latest innovations.

Then, I attend in-person events monthly and meet and greet people from different generations, sectors and backgrounds. And I don't wait to be invited, either. I find, seek and ask around. I join waitlists and buy tickets. And when it is logistically possible, I go to six or seven events — and yes, I always wear pink.

Your brand isn't merely about your advancement — it's about creating pathways for every woman and girl who follows. In a world demanding women stay quiet and grateful, your brand becomes a protest sign. Every post, every presentation and every public appearance becomes a strategic strike against systemic oppression. Remember — this is about creating a new normal where future generations of women won't have to choose between being professional and being themselves. Wear the colour, share the story, claim the space and keep the accent.

Points For Reflection

How might your story empower others?

What is stopping you from being visible?

What would you discuss publicly if you were not afraid?

"I learned a long time ago that the wisest thing I can do is be on my own side, be an advocate for myself and others like me."

Maya Angelou

Meet The Author

Beverley McPherson is a Speaker and Mentor dedicated to helping individuals break free from the people-pleasing cycle. With years of life experience and a deep understanding of personal growth, she empowers others to set healthy boundaries, reclaim their confidence and prioritise their needs without guilt. Through compassionate guidance and practical strategies, Beverley shows how to live authentically and create more meaningful, balanced relationships. Beverley was a consummate people-pleaser with shifting identities, surrendering control to others. The last 10 years have been spent learning to create and maintain boundaries, control the narrative and own her Yes.

Stepping Out Of The Shadows

Beverley McPherson

In this chapter, Beverley describes her fear of networking and how an empowering cup of coffee gave her the confidence to rescue herself from a life in the shadows.

When walking into a networking event, do you ever wonder how some people manage to stride confidently into a room full of strangers and introduce themselves with ease? It's a skill I've admired for years and certainly not one I ever felt easy with. There are so many times when I've asked myself what on earth I'm doing here and wanted instead to be at home with my feet up watching an action movie.

I remember a particular night. I walked into a networking event that almost broke me. I can still see it vividly, the black curtained walls with dark corners and the occasional glittering flash of light.

Picture this. The room roars with conversation — everyone seems to be talking at once. No one appears to be listening. There's smiling, mingling and air kisses. The wine flows and glasses clink.

The room is buzzing with energy, with an occasional burst of laughter heard above the chatter.

The lights are low and jazz is playing quietly in the background. The air is heavy with perfume and everything is glittering. Everyone looks stunning.

And there in the corner, watching, envying the effortless getting-to-know-you conversations, a woman stands alone.

Present, yet absent.

Scared and fighting a battle she knows she cannot afford to lose — the outcome of which could mean the difference between living and existing. It's taken all her courage just to be in the room, in the corner, in the shadows.

Barely holding on, nausea rising, ears ringing — every fibre of her being screams at her to leave, to turn on her heels, to run for her life. Her struggle is real.

Scared to be seen, scared to be heard, scared to be spoken to and scared to live.

Her fear immobilises her, leaving her only able to complete what she is required to do.

She waits.

Waits for someone to say, "Come on in, the water's fine."

But nobody does.

That scared woman in the shadows?

That was me at one of the many networking events happening each week. Finally, plucking up the courage to attend but hiding in the corner.

I was terrified. Gripped by the fear of how I would be perceived by anyone I spoke to. Maybe people would think I was stupid with nothing to contribute to their conversations.

I was so afraid of being judged — I would do nothing to draw attention to myself.

Sometimes, people would mock me in a passive-aggressive way and inside I would be seething but would bite my tongue and laugh along.

The truth is, I wanted to be heard. I wanted to be seen.

I wanted to be involved.

I wanted to get out there and do things.

Instead, I was hiding in a corner, not living. I felt I was merely existing.

Waiting for permission.

But permission from who?

No matter which direction I looked, no one was coming to rescue me. There was no handsome prince.

I had to rescue myself.

As a senior leader, I was confident, respected and in control. I was employed in the male-dominated construction, law, oil and gas industries. In my professional life, I could hold my own, but in my personal life, I shrank back into the shadows and hid until it was time to return to work.

The catalyst for my change was dark and completely irrational. It came unexpectedly at a low point in my life. I was sitting on the edge of the bed calculating how much time I had left, based on my age, before I died and I would finally be free. I caught myself in this thought, shocked to the core.

I wasn't really wishing myself dead, but wishing I had the courage to walk away from the life I was living.

It was not a good place to be.

And that was it. The beginning. I realised I had to do something. To change.

I asked myself, "Beverley, do you want to spend the rest of your life in pain?"

Physical pain. Pain that seemed to feed on the pain it created. A vicious circle.

The answer was no.

I was mentally exhausted from holding it all in and keeping my mouth shut, allowing others to do and say what they wanted. Sometimes, I wanted to scream and shout, "Shut up, leave me alone," but I didn't.

I was emotionally exhausted from supporting everyone else while hiding my emotional turmoil. All the while, a simmering anger was held in check.

I was stressed. Adrenaline constantly poured into my system every waking moment. Living in a perpetual state of fight or flight.

How many of us know what it's like to feel ourselves sinking with nothing to hold onto? Knowing that if we don't take action, we may reach a place of no return.

I knew I was the only one who could change my life and my environment. To do it, drastic action was needed. So, in desperation to save myself and find who I was, I ran.

I booked a flight to Dubai, a place I had lived happily for 17 years before returning to the UK in 2013. I had had enough and thought a return to Dubai would help. And it did.

The journey to finding your voice begins when you say, "enough is enough" and take the first small steps forward. Until then, you will continue to settle.

Three things can help you on your journey.

Firstly, to move on without ever settling again, you must decide how to show up for yourself authentically.

But let's be clear — being authentic and showing up as you means more than simply turning up.

It's about how you see yourself and want others to see you.

It's about every aspect of your life.

We hear a lot about personal branding and authenticity. But I've learned it's really about being yourself in how you dress, speak, think and set boundaries to support who you are becoming. Don't let others live your life through yours vicariously. Take control and be comfortable and confident with this.

It's finding more than your voice. So, what is your gut saying about who you are?

Secondly, the journey to find your voice is much easier when you have support — someone in your corner who will hold you accountable. To share the load and a place to rest when you need to take a breath, gather your thoughts and strength. After all, personal change and learning to honour yourself is hard work.

This is not a journey you can take alone. It's you versus you. Your mindset, beliefs and fears all come into play.

Thirdly, what do you see people doing that you'd love to do but are too scared to try and don't know why? Maybe it's irrational. All you know is that the thought of doing it sends your heart rate racing.

I'll share what mine was. Believe it or not, it was having coffee on my own in public. It was that small and simple. Yet I felt I would be judged and stared at for doing it.

To overcome this, I began with a small, brave step. I bought a coffee and walked on the beach — no one stared. The next time, I sat on a bench beside a lake — no one paid any attention. And finally, I sat inside the coffee shop and read a book. Realising what a gift it was to have this time — that no one was staring and there was nothing to be scared of was a beautiful, empowering moment that changed my life.

In the movie *The Greatest Showman*, there's a song the bearded lady sings, 'This Is Me' and the line I love about being unapologetically me has become my mantra.

Because I am no longer afraid to be seen, I no longer apologise for who I am because now I am me.

I had been quiet for way too long.

Now, I attend networking events, which still scare me a little, but I no longer hover in the corner or around the edge of conversation groups. Instead, I comment, interact and confidently share who I am.

Small, brave steps. Being real. Asking for help. Doing what scares you. That's how you leave the corner, step fully into your light and take ownership of your voice.

Points For Reflection

What word can you use to describe yourself, the authentic you? It may help to think of this as a word you would like others to use to describe you. What is the outcome and what do they do with the information?

Who can you ask for support? As the old adage says, a problem shared is a problem halved, so who will be in your corner to keep you on track?

What do you see others doing that you would love to do that scares you? Like my coffee at the beach, what's the first step you can take to make this a reality?

Meet The Author

Margarita Giles-Martinez is a Purpose Coach, Speaker and Co-founder of Woman's Search for Meaning. She helps women reconnect with WHO they are and WHY they're here so they can live with clarity, confidence, authenticity and deep fulfilment. Women who work with Margarita often move from feeling stuck or disconnected to living lives rooted in meaning and aligned with their true selves. Through her coaching, retreats and talks, she creates spaces for lasting transformation — where women rediscover their voice, awaken their purpose and step into the fullness of who they're meant to be.

Unshakeable — You Were Never Meant To Fit In

Margarita Giles-Martinez

Margarita invites us to rewrite the script in a world that rewards conformity. This chapter is a rallying cry for anyone who has ever felt not good enough or struggled with confidence — reminding us that true confidence isn't about fitting in or performing but about remembering who we truly are.

From a young age, we're taught that acceptance comes with conditions. Be polite. Be smart. Be strong, but not too strong. Wear what's in, say what's safe and do what's expected.

It's no wonder so many of us shape-shift through life, trimming parts of ourselves to fit into spaces never designed for our whole selves.

The result is a slow, quiet disconnection from our authenticity and our truth. And when you're disconnected, confidence can't thrive. Not because you're not good enough but because you're not rooted in who you really are.

This is why even the most outwardly successful people struggle with public speaking, relationships, or simply being visible.

How can your voice ever feel real if you're performing someone else's script?

In the mid-2010s, I was working at my family's marketing agency. From the outside, it looked like success — high-profile clients in London and the US, polished presentations, glowing accounts and endless smiles through every pitch.

But inside, I was shrinking. Not because I was shy but because I was selling projects I had no passion for. Every time I stepped on a stage or sat in a meeting, it felt like my voice was borrowed.

Eventually, I hit a wall. What began as quiet burnout gradually cracked open into a full-blown identity crisis. I couldn't keep pretending.

So, I had to walk away.

I retrained as a life coach and within weeks of certification, I was running workshops for women on alignment and authentic living. I was still speaking, but the energy was different.

I wasn't performing anymore. I was serving.

And something extraordinary happened. Confidence showed up, not as a performance, but as a byproduct of authenticity.

Through this, I've learned what unshakeable confidence looks like.

It's not about more. More qualifications. More polish. More applause. It's about less. Less pretending. Less hiding. Less compromise. It's available to anyone — not because we earn it, but because we remember it.

Unshakeable confidence is born from alignment.

It begins by knowing WHO you are, WHY you're here, and HOW to serve.

Here's how to start reconnecting with that core.

First, you need to reconnect with who you are. Before the world told you who to be, you were the curious, intuitive, alive version of yourself. That version still lives in you. She's just been buried under years of conditioning.

What did you love doing before anyone told you what success looked like? What makes you feel most alive, even when no one's watching? What would you do differently today if failure wasn't a factor and no one was judging?

These aren't just journaling prompts. They're breadcrumbs back to yourself.

Be ready, though — this process often stirs up beliefs that keep us stuck. You may find yourself confronting ideas about what's realistic, practical or desirable. That's a good thing.

Growth begins where conditioning ends.

I remember sitting in a boardroom in London, surrounded by executives, feeling like I knew all the right things to say. I had rehearsed the spiel a hundred times. But whenever someone asked a question - something I wasn't expecting, I would freeze inside.

I second-guessed every word before it left my mouth, terrified of being exposed as a fraud. In that room, I realised that no matter how well I played the part, it wasn't me speaking. And until I reconnected with the real version of myself — the one who didn't need a script — confidence would always feel out of reach.

To uncover your why, you don't need to change your entire life overnight. Start small.

Create pockets of time where you do what makes you feel most alive. Once a week or once a month is enough.

It doesn't have to be dramatic to be meaningful. It just needs to be true.

When you honour yourself in these small, consistent ways, something powerful begins to happen. You start to see that what lights you up isn't just for you. It can serve others, too.

I've seen this unfold not just in my own life but in the lives of many women I've had the privilege of coaching.

One woman discovered she had a natural ability to connect deeply with strangers, making people feel truly seen and heard. Once she stopped brushing it off as 'just being friendly', she realised she was born to help others transform and launched her career as a transformational consultant.

Another client, an estate agent who sang as a hobby, realised that people weren't just entertained through her music. They were healing. They were reconnecting with their hearts. And she knew then that performing wasn't just a dream. It was her duty.

When you keep showing up for what you love, something shifts. Your why begins to take shape — not through striving, but through service.

By being your authentic self, using your gifts and experiences to contribute something meaningful to others.

Your why isn't something you chase. You uncover it by being faithful to who you already are.

Unshakeable confidence is harvested by rooting your voice and work in your why — the deepest reason behind what you do. From that place, you begin to reconnect with your unique how — your personal way of serving others.

When you adopt this approach, the fear of being judged starts to dissolve because now, it's not about you. It's about the impact you're here to make.

Your how doesn't have to look dramatic or charitable to be powerful. Sometimes, it's simply about creating a product or service that makes life easier for someone, telling a story that helps someone feel less alone, or offering a service that uplifts, inspires, or heals.

All it has to do is add value to others. All it has to do is serve.

When your voice becomes an extension of your truth, you stop worrying about perfecting it because you're no longer performing. You're offering. And in that offering, confidence finds you.

Over the years, I've witnessed extraordinary transformations when women harvest unshakeable confidence by finding alignment with who they are, why they're here and how they're here to serve.

Clients have walked away from successful corporate careers to pursue their art. Women have left emotionally abusive relationships after reconnecting with their worth. Others have simply stopped 'living by the rules' and started following their hearts — setting boundaries, choosing alignment and finally claiming their voice.

And in every single case, the shift didn't come from perfection. It came from truth. From choosing to live and speak from their why.

Watching these women rise — not just in confidence, but in self-respect, reminds me daily why I do this work. This is what purpose looks like in action.

Never forget that the world needs your voice.

Not everyone will resonate with your truth. And that's okay.

You're not here to speak to everyone.

You're here to speak to someone.

And that someone is waiting for your message, story, light.

You don't need to be flawless.

You just need to be real.

The world isn't waiting for perfect.

It's waiting for you.

Points For Reflection

What would your life look like if no one was watching and fear didn't exist?

Block out one hour a week to do something that makes you feel alive just for you. No performance.

No productivity goals. Just you, your joy and your truth. What begins as an hour can become a way of life.

Think of one person whose life might change if you fully share your voice, work, or story. Let them become your focus, not your fear.

Meet The Author

Kathleen Cornmell is a qualified Nutritionist, Energy and Hormone Specialist, passionate about helping women restore their energy and rebalance their hormones through practical lifestyle and nutrition strategies. After experiencing debilitating fatigue, chronic pain and burnout in her thirties, Kathleen left her engineering career to rebuild her health and her life. Now, she empowers women to stop surviving and start thriving through clinical work and speaking. Her approach is rooted in lived experience, science and deep empathy, with one mission — to help women reclaim their vitality, joy and confidence through nutritional and lifestyle medicine.

Fatigue To Fabulous — Finding Myself Again

Kathleen Cornmell

Kathleen shares the personal burnout that changed her life and the practical strategies she now uses to help women restore their energy, rebalance hormones and feel like themselves again.

I remember sitting on the hallway floor, crying because I didn't have the energy to take my son to school.

This feeling wasn't just tiredness but complete exhaustion, for which no amount of sleep helped. I was in constant pain, my head pounded and I felt like the light inside me had gone out. I was cancelling plans, missing time with my children and hardly making it through each day. I felt like a failure, as a mum, a wife, a woman, constantly scared when my husband left for work.

How could I do everything I needed to do?

Every time I missed a day out, every time I said, "Mummy's too tired today", it chipped away at who I was meant to be.

I was in my thirties. I was supposed to be thriving. Instead, I felt like a stranger in my own body.

That moment on the floor changed everything. I realised that no one was coming to fix it. My doctors had let me down and left me to cope alone. I had to take control.

So, I did. I started researching (not easy pre-Instagram or Facebook), learning, testing and rebuilding my strength. I changed my food habits and lifestyle. Slowly, I began to feel like me again.

That experience didn't just heal me. It changed the direction of my life, career and the well-being of my family. I left engineering and became a nutritionist to help other women reclaim their lives, just as I had. There is nothing like taking control of your life to feel empowered and healthy.

Let's start at the beginning. What is energy?

At a biological level, energy comes from Adenosine Triphosphate (ATP), your cells' internal battery. To make ATP, your body needs macronutrients — carbohydrates, fats and proteins. These are the raw materials for power production.

But here's where it goes wrong. Most of us are fueling on quick fixes — carbohydrates such as cereal, toast, coffee and sugar. They work in the moment, giving you a short burst of energy, but a hard crash swiftly follows.

This blood sugar crash triggers cortisol, your primary stress hormone, which sends your body into survival mode. When you live in that mode long-term, everything suffers — your mood, motivation, immune system and especially your hormones. Your body prioritises cortisol production over other hormones (such oestrogen, progesterone and testosterone) because they share common building blocks. Your body diverts resources away from reproductive hormones to meet the demands that stress places on it. Over time, this can lead to imbalances like irregular cycles, low libido, premenstrual syndrome, menopausal symptoms or even fertility issues.

When you're constantly on a blood sugar rollercoaster, your energy crashes aren't just tiring. They're disrupting your entire hormonal system.

So, how do we stop the cycle?

I use six core strategies to overcome chronic fatigue and achieve consistent energy. Adopting these will help you move from fatigue to fabulous and feel empowered.

Firstly, one of the most powerful shifts you can make is how you start your day.

A typical Western breakfast is high in carbohydrates — toast, cereal, fruit juice and coffee. These spike your blood sugar and lead to an energy dip a few hours later. You might find yourself reaching for more sugar, more caffeine or feeling like you need a nap. Setting you up for a blood sugar rollercoaster.

Instead, aim for a breakfast rich in protein and healthy fats. Think eggs with avocado, Greek yoghurt with seeds, a smoothie with protein powder and nut butter.

Protein and fat help stabilise your blood sugar and reduce cortisol spikes, which support your hormone balance throughout the day.

Also, never eat a naked carb. Always pair carbohydrates with protein or fat to reduce blood sugar spikes.

If you want to dive deeper into this topic, the book *The Glucose Goddess Method* is brilliant and full of helpful tips.[1]

If you continue this theme with lunch and dinner, your blood sugar and therefore, your energy will remain steady throughout the day.

Secondly, your body needs a range of vitamins and minerals beyond macronutrients to create energy and regulate hormones. Key players here include B vitamins, magnesium and vitamin D.

These support your ATP production and nervous system. Without them, your body can't function efficiently.

A simple solution is to eat the rainbow. The more colour on your plate, the better. Each colour provides different nutrients to support your energy, mood and immunity.

My third strategy is to prioritise quality sleep. It sounds basic, but sleep is non-negotiable if you want to feel good.

Lack of sleep raises cortisol for the whole day, disrupting hormones, impairing digestion and increasing sugar cravings. It also affects the gut microbiome, home to good bacteria that regulate mood and energy.

Did you know that a staggering 68% of people in the West struggle with sleep?[2]

If that's you, try these tried and tested ideas.

Stick to a regular bedtime — even on weekends.

Set an evening alarm to remind you it's time to go to bed.

Get outside during the day as natural light helps produce melatonin, your sleep hormone.

Avoid eating too close to bedtime.

Track your sleep using a wearable device — I love the Oura Ring as it keeps me accountable.[3]

Some traditions, such as Vastu Shastra (India's equivalent of Feng Shui), suggest sleeping with your head pointing south, which may align you better with the Earth's natural energy flow, supporting better rest and sleep.[4]

Also, limit caffeine intake and have your last cup no later than 10 hours before bed, ideally.

Fourthly, we need to talk about stress. We can't avoid it altogether, but we can learn to manage it better.

When stressed, your body releases glucose into the bloodstream to provide energy to fight or flee. This spikes your blood sugar, triggering a rollercoaster of highs and crashes.

Over time, chronic stress depletes your hormones, immunity, energy and emotional resilience.

So, be sure to build in daily habits that help you reset, including the following.

Breathing exercises or meditation.

Journaling.

Exercise — anything from walking to weight training, whatever works for you.

Saying 'no' more often. As women, we usually take on too much.

Even small things, like ten minutes of quiet time, can shift your body out of fight-or-flight and into rest-and-digest. Use apps like Calm or Headspace.

Next, my fifth strategy is the simplest of tips and one of the most powerful. It's about water.

Water is essential for energy. Your cells need it to make ATP, your brain needs it to focus and your body needs it to detox. Yet 75% of people are chronically dehydrated.[5]

Aim for around two litres of water daily, more if you're active. Sip throughout the day rather than chugging it all at once.

If plain water feels boring, add a slice of lemon, cucumber or fresh mint. Keep a bottle with you as a visual reminder to drink.

My sixth tip is to look at your relationship with caffeine.

I used to think coffee was my best friend. It gave me the boost I craved in the morning, or at least I thought it did.

But caffeine stimulates cortisol, creating the same stress response over and over. It also affects your blood sugar and disrupts sleep, even if you drink it early in the day.

Try cutting back to one coffee in the morning, or use a high-quality decaf. Ideally, take a break from it for a few weeks to see how you feel. When caffeine is eliminated or reduced, you may notice less anxiety, better sleep and more stable energy.

Making just a few simple, targeted changes can transform how you feel physically, emotionally and mentally. I've lived at both ends of the spectrum, from flat-out fatigue to full-on fabulous and I promise, the climb back is worth it.

Start with one change. Then another. Before long, you'll remember what it feels like to wake up empowered and excited for your day.

Fatigue isn't your destiny, and you deserve to feel fabulous!

Points For Reflection

What's draining your energy most right now and what's one small way you can change it?

When do you feel most like yourself? What routines, food or environments help you feel that way?

What would you do with your energy if you had more of it? What becomes possible?

Meet The Author

Gill McKay is a Sobriety Guide and Educator, coaching successful professionals to break free from the hold of drinking, find their alcohol-free voice and start living a life on their terms. With a background in neuroscience, Gill is also an award-winning TEDx speaker and best-selling author of *STUCK: Brain Smart Insights for Coaches.* Gill is a qualified Executive Coach and Group Facilitator and has worked with hundreds of clients to increase their confidence in communications and public speaking, to overcome imposter syndrome, become comfortable in their own skin, share their stories with a positive mindset and recognise that their voice matters.

Unapologetically Me — Why Being Comfortable In Your Own Skin Is The Real Superpower

Gill McKay

Gill writes about how her experience of feeling different has influenced her life, her brief affair with 'comparisonitis' and how being a rebellious, intuitive outlier has shaped the way she shows up in the world, for herself and within all her relationships.

Have you ever felt like an outlier, someone on the edges of the action, someone who doesn't quite fit in? It can certainly be a lonely place at times. However, it can also be a place of deep awareness — and if we can be present to it, being that outsider can bring profound moments of clarity, strength and empowerment. There really is nothing like being comfortable in your skin — yet it can be a messy journey to get there.

Last year in May, my daughter Ellie ran the Copenhagen marathon to raise money for Great Ormond Street Hospital. Jogging between various viewing points, I was dripping with pride at her commitment, drive and purpose. She not only smashed her target time, finishing in 3 hours 41 minutes, but also reached the massive fundraising goal of £1,974.

That number — 1974 — represented the year I underwent a complicated heart operation to repair a large hole between my two ventricles. These days, due to incredible medical advances, the surgery is not just more frequent but also significantly safer and more successful. I am forever grateful to my parents for making the decision to say yes to what proved to be life-saving surgery and having the courage to take what was, in those days, a real risk.

My heart condition meant I was small, with a slight blueish tone, most noticeable on my lips and my nails — due to the lower oxygenation of my blood through my malformed heart. Rather surprisingly, I was also super strong and energetic, with a love of gymnastics and adventurous ice skating — and my parents had a challenging time dealing with their go-getting young daughter whilst underneath it all wanting to wrap me in kid gloves.

I knew from an early age that I was different. Even before I 'clocked' the regular hospital check-ups weren't something my sister and brother had to endure, there was something in the tone of the way people spoke to me, gently, almost forgivingly, overly encouraging. Often being told I was special.

Thank goodness I didn't become a difficult 'princess child' — which could have been the result of being frequently told I was extraordinary. My wonderful late mum often told a story of when I was four, after a hospital visit, taking me to a café for my treat meal of beans on toast. When telling me I was special, I retorted. "But Mum, we are all special. We just have to find out our own special thing."

I always believed that from a young age — and still do. Knowing who you are, your strengths and your values helps you find your place in the world, your purpose, your contribution and ultimately, your legacy.

As a child, I was really OK with being different, being the girl on half-day schooling, the girl with the holey heart, the girl with the spindly legs and the girl with blue lips. I never felt I missed out and being nurtured and loved by a busy family paved the way for my quiet confidence with friends at school, at the skating rink and at the gymnastics club. Looking back, it wasn't just my health that brought difference, but also the make-up of my family. I was lucky to live in a three-generational household, alongside my paternal grandmother, my parents and brother and sister. My parents were doctors and my dad specialised in obstetrics and gynaecology, so there were always fascinating conversations at the dinner table. We talked openly about many topics and had so much fun teasing each other. My mum always managed to spin the meal to a few more plates to enable friends to stay to eat. I have definitely inherited that open-house approach from her!

I was never one of the 'popular' girls but was really OK with that. I was happy with my friends Cathy and Karen, both of whom, as adults, discussed their sense of feeling different as youngsters, too. Sadly, Cathy died eight years ago and I miss her acerbic wit so much but am hugely grateful to be godmother to her twin daughters. And I still enjoy a good old natter with Karen on long walks in Richmond Park a few times a year.

It may seem a strange thing to read, however, I feel really lucky to have been born with a heart defect as it inevitably created my reality and the imprint of who I would become as a woman in the future.

I feel lucky to have learned at such a young age there are some things in life I just couldn't control, so it made sense to work with what I had, not resent what I didn't.

I feel lucky I learned to trust myself as a child and tap into my intuition of what would work for me, knowing I was loved and safe in my family environment and with my friends.

And I feel lucky to be genuinely comfortable being me in my own skin, even though it had a slightly pale blue tone at times!

Of course, life wasn't all plain sailing. I still experienced the inevitable hormonal 'joys' of the teenage years but seemed to weather it rather well, grateful for my newfound health after my heart surgery. I recall a particularly challenging conversation with my parents at 16, being the only one of their kids who enjoyed science at school, about the possibility of studying medicine at university. There was the underlying 'hint' about giving back to the medical profession for my gift of life, yet I knew within every bone of my body that I wouldn't be a great doctor like my parents were. Even at that young age, I knew my empath nature and compassionate personality could lead to a problem of attachment to patients — something that has borne out in later life as a coach, for which I still work with a supervisor.

And that is a critical lesson — knowing what you are not or don't want is just as important as knowing who you are and what you do want. How many times have you said yes because of someone else's expectations? At 16, I trusted my intuition enough to have an adult conversation with my parents about my career, even knowing it would disappoint them. I now know that self-trust is a gift.

However, in my late 20s, my world was turned upside down when I had a visit from the self-doubt gremlins and I no longer felt OK being me. My first husband had an affair with a good friend (for clarity, not Cathy or Karen), a friend who I persuaded him to move into our house as she was going through a dreadful split up at the time. Yes, that's the compassionate empath in action! As the story unfolded, I found out that the affair wasn't just for a few weeks but had gone on for more than 18 months. I was rocked to the core by the lies and the betrayal and by the fact that my husband and I had been trying for a baby all through this period.

And it didn't help that she was a willowy supermodel lookalike! My whole sense of self was knocked, from the perspective of how I looked and who I was. For the first time, I didn't feel I was enough. I lived in a world of comparison. What did she have that I didn't? Why couldn't I be more like her? Why did he feel the need to stray? I challenged everything about how I lived my life, often through a haze of bottles of cheap wine, scores of Silk Cut cigarettes and tearful, ranting evenings with my incredible friends.

Then, one day, I left my smoky, boozy home to visit my parents and immediately felt safe again. My brother, sister and their partners visited and it felt like old times. And within that safety, I found me again, the real me. I knew what I was made of and knew I would heal. Most importantly, I knew I was enough.

And I was happy being me — I didn't want to be a willowy supermodel lookalike with a lying new partner. With my fabulous family and friends,

I was happy being the real me —the 5-foot-5-inch, average-height, empathic, compassionate woman. I was once again comfortable in my own skin, living an aligned life.

And the best bit about this story? I had decided to spend a year being a party girl and dating many guys, as I had always been in a long-term relationship. Well, that didn't work out as I met my now husband (of nearly 30 years) within three weeks of partying and intuitively knew it was right. He did, too, as he was as comfortable in his own skin as I was in mine!

I am grateful to my imperfect, broken heart in so many ways. Its story has always been a gift, and I now recognise that it isn't just the pump of my life force, but also of my empowerment. I now work with other women to help them become empowered and happy with who they are, find their voice and show up in the world authentically comfortable in their own skin.

And remember this from a four-year-old. We are all special. We just need to find our special thing. What's yours?

Points For Reflection

When have you trusted your intuition, and how can you tap into it more?

When do you feel in flow and how can you do more of it?

What words would you use to describe your strengths? What makes you uniquely special?

"What we know matters, but who we are matters more."

Brené Brown

Conclusion

Kier Adair and Gill McKay

How to sum up a book of such magnitude? Well maybe start with just one word – WOW!

Congratulations to each and every one of our authors, for sharing their voices with authenticity, courage, vulnerability and honesty and for being catalysts for hope and new ways of thinking.

The chapters in this book offer many different lessons, yet they are all linked by the golden thread of the theme of empowerment. Empowering women to rise, take a stand and claim their space in the world.

We encourage you to take your time to reflect on the three points at the end of each chapter, to journal your thoughts and use them as prompts if ever you feel stuck. Revisit the chapters again for inspiration and ideas and make sure you connect with the authors via their individual QR codes to follow more of their content and thought leadership.

And finally, thank you for being part of the Speak and Shine movement by reading our first collaboration book. We know it is the first of many more to come.

Empowering you to rise!

Kier and Gill

Acknowledgements

Thank you for joining us in celebrating the brilliance in *Empowering Women To Rise.*

Thank you to every speaker who said yes to themselves and bravely took to our stage to share their voice, without whom Speak and Shine would not exist.

To everyone who has supported Speak and Shine, from panellists and keynotes to audience members who have attended events, brought their vibrant energy and contributed to the beautiful experience.

And those that have shown up online in the same positive way through our Speak and Shine Membership and Speak and Shine Connector, as well as liking and commenting on posts to create the momentum that helped grow a little idea into a big deal.

The fabulous Kirsty Carden for trusting and partnering with us from the outset to give our speakers and audience a brilliant next step to level-up. For her brilliant advice and encouragement to strive for more.

Amanda FitzGerald for always encouraging us to own our worth and take The Speak and Shine Collection to the next level with media support. Thank you for being there from the start, from panellist to speaker at our Summits.

To Kay Korsh who gave incredible styling advice and guidance to our speakers to gain more and more confidence for their moment. She too rocked our stage as a panellist in December and will always be our 'Bond Girl'!

To Lenny Oguntade and his team of videographers — Jay Notley and Courtney Andrews for their patience and creativity in finding the light in every occasion.

And John Carden for his tenacity in delivering show-stopping speaker reels for our clients, who are now making waves in the speaker world, armed with their authority assets.

Barbara Sylvester, Angela Geldenhuys and Fran Robinson for capturing those magic in the moment shots and giving us beautiful imagery to share our stories.

We are hugely grateful to Anna Sigolotto and her team at Kindred for the stunning space and service that we always receive that make our events boujee and beautiful.

Together with their resident AV wizard Kevin Sones, who worked his magic and bonded with our creative team.

Katy Barrett from The W Collective for her thoughtful and luxurious speaker gifts; Anne Nicholls for her generous donation of her dignity bags as goodie bags; and Dani Marcos at FASTSIGNS for creating and gifting name badges at the 11th hour. All making the December Summit so special.

To Trudie Avery for the stunningly beautiful artwork you see on the cover. She totally understood our essence and delivered to our brief in record time.

Julie Brown for her incredible knowledge and hard work in creating this wonderful book and coaching us through the publishing process.

And finally, for the love and support of our family and friends who have been there through the rollercoaster (but beautiful) ride of birthing this book.

A heartfelt thank you to you all for making Speak and Shine the movement it is.

References

Introduction

1: Elrod, H. (2019) *The Miracle Equation*. London: Hachette UK.

Marie Fraser

1: Daily Brit NewsDesk. (2024) 'Women Spend 21 Years Of Their Life On A Diet', *The Daily Brit*, 8 March. Available at: https://thedailybrit.co.uk/women-spend-21-years-of-their-life-on-a-diet/ (Accessed: 22 May 2025).

2: Walker, C. (2021) 'Waist of Money: UK adults spend £20,000 on weight loss tactics over a lifetime', *benendenhealth*, 13 December. Available at: https://www.benenden.co.uk/newsroom/diet-and-nutrition/ (Accessed: 23 May 2025).

3: de Cabo, R. and Mattson, M.P. (2019) 'Effects of Intermittent Fasting on Health, Aging, and Disease', *New England Journal of Medicine*, 381(26), pp. 2541–2551. doi: https://doi.org/10.1056/nejmra1905136

4: Pelz, M. (2022) *Fast Like a Girl*. California: Hay House, Inc.

Nessa O'Gorman

1: Auxier, B., Anderson, M., Perrin, A. and Turner, E. (2020) 'Parenting Children in the Age of Screens', *Pew Research Center*, 28 July. Available at: https://www.pewresearch.org/internet/2020/07/28/parenting-children-in-the-age-of-screens/ (Accessed: 23 May 2025).

Sharon Eden

1: Miller, L. (2021) *The Awakened Brain: The Psychology of Spirituality*. London: Penguin Random House UK.

Katja Brodt de Sousa

1: Campaign to End Loneliness. (2024) *Facts and statistics about loneliness*. Available at: https://www.campaigntoendloneliness.org/facts-and-statistics/ (Accessed: 22 May 2025).

2: His Holiness the 14th Dalai Lama. (2020) *Establishing Harmony within Religious Diversity*. Available at: https://www.dalailama.com/messages/religious-harmony-1/establishing-harmony-within-religious-diversity (Accessed: 22 May 2025).

Karen Farrell

1: Hendricks, G. (2010) *The Big Leap*. New York: Harper Collins.

2: Huberman Lab. (2023) 'Breathwork Protocols for Health, Focus & Stress', *Huberman Lab*, 6 October. Available at: https://www.hubermanlab.com/newsletter/breathwork-protocols-for-health-focus-stress (Accessed: 22 May 2025).

Ann Marie Cunningham

1: Tolle, E. (2003) *Stillness Speaks: Whispers of Now*. California: New World Library.

2: Van der Kolk, B. A. (2015) *The body keeps the score: Mind, brain and body in the transformation of trauma*. London: Penguin Books Ltd.

3: Maté, G. and Maté, D. (2022) *The myth of normal: Trauma, illness, and healing in a toxic culture*. New York: Avery.

4: Phelan, V. (2019) *Overcoming: A memoir*. Dublin: Hachette Books Ireland.

5: Angelou, M. (1969) *I know why the caged bird sings*. New York: Random House.

Rebecca Leppard

1: Eunson, B. (2020) 'Gender and Communication' in Eunson, B. (ed.) *C21 Communicating In The 21st Century*. 4th edn. New York: Wiley.

2: Silman, A. (2025) Now comes the 'womanosphere': the anti-feminist media telling women to be thin, fertile and Republican, *The Guardian*, 24 April. Available at: https://www.theguardian.com/us-news/2025/apr/24/womanosphere-conservative-women (Accessed: 22 May 2025).

3: Wikipedia. (2019) *Child marriage in the United States*. Available at: https://en.wikipedia.org/wiki/Child_marriage_in_the_United_States (Accessed: 22 May 2025).

4: Collins, R. and PA Media. (2023) 'Mother jailed for taking abortion pills after legal limit', *BBC News*, 12 June. Available at: https://www.bbc.co.uk/news/uk-england-stoke-staffordshire-65882169 (Accessed: 22 May 2025).

5: Baird, V. (2022) 'The distressing truth is that if you are raped in Britain today, your chances of seeing justice are slim', *Victims Commissioner*, 21 June. Available at: https://victimscommissioner.org.uk/news/the-distressing-truth-is-that-if-you-are-raped-in-britain-today-your-chances-of-seeing-justice-are-slim/ (Accessed: 22 May 2025).

6: United Nations Office On Drugs and Crime. (2024) *Femicides in 2023 Global estimates of intimate partner/family member femicides*. Available at: https://www.unodc.org/documents/data-and-analysis/briefs/Femicide_Brief_2024.pdf (Accessed: 22 May 2025).

7: Amnesty International UK. (2025) 'Toxic tech: New polling exposes widespread online misogyny driving Gen Z away from social media', *Amnesty International*, 21 March. Available at: https://www.amnesty.org.uk/press-releases/toxic-tech-new-polling-exposes-widespread-online-misogyny-driving-gen-z-away-social (Accessed: 22 May 2025).

8: Hustlers University. (2023) *Hustlers University*. Available at: https://hustlers-university.ca/ (Accessed: 24 May 2025).

9: Mohammed, K. (2025) 'Emboldened by Trump, the 'liberal' UK is giving free rein to its colonial impulses', *The Guardian*, 21 April. Available at: https://www.theguardian.com/global-development/2025/apr/21/caribbean-trump-democracy-colonialism-liberal-uk-immigration-us-cuba-commonwealth (Accessed: 22 May 2025).

10: Lane, C. (2024) 'Social Media Algorithms Amplify Misogynistic Content to Teens', *UCL News*, 5 February. Available at: https://www.ucl.ac.uk/news/2024/feb/social-media-algorithms-amplify-misogynistic-content-teens (Accessed: 22 May 2025).

11: Oxford Internet Institute. (2024) *Internet use statistically associated with higher wellbeing, finds new global Oxford study*. Available at: https://www.oii.ox.ac.uk/news-events/internet-use-statistically-associated-with-higher-wellbeing-finds-new-global-oxford-study/ (Accessed: 22 May 2025).

Kathleen Cornmell

1: Inchauspé, J. (2023) *The Glucose Goddess Method: Your four-week guide to cutting cravings, getting your energy back, and feeling amazing.* New York: Simon & Schuster.

2: Dinic, M. (2022) *The YouGov Sleep Study.* Available at: https://yougov.co.uk/health/articles/42957-yougov-sleep-study (Accessed: 22 May 2025).

3: Oura. (2024) *Oura Ring.* Available at: https://ouraring.com (Accessed: 22 May 2025).

4: Summer, J.V. (2021) *Which Direction is Best to Sleep in?* Available at: https://www.sleepfoundation.org/sleeping-positions/best-direction-to-sleep (Accessed: 22 May 2025).

5: Office for National Statistics. (2021) *Three-quarters of Adults in Great Britain Worry about Climate Change*. Available at: https://www.ons.gov.uk/peoplepopulationandcommunity/wellbeing/articles/threequartersofadultsingreatbritainworryaboutclimatechange/2021-11-05 (Accessed: 22 May 2025).

Printed in Dunstable, United Kingdom

64371481R00117